THE
ILLUSTRATED HISTORY OF WEAPONS
RIFLES

KINGSFORDEDITIONS

Distributed by Kingsford Editions
45–55 Fairchild Street
Heatherton Victoria 3202 Australia
www.hinkler.com.au

Copyright © Hinkler Books Pty Ltd 2014

Created by Moseley Road Inc.
President: Sean Moore
Project art and editorial director: Tina Vaughan and Damien Moore
Editor: Lesley Malkin
Cover design: Hinkler Design Studio
Internal design: Mark Johnson-Davies,
Andy Crisp, Kate Stretton, Philippa Baile
Photographer: Jonathan Conklin Photography, Inc.
f-stop fitzgerald
Author: Rupert Matthews
Prepress: Graphic Print Group

ISBN: 978 1 7436 3057 0

Printed and bound in China

THE
ILLUSTRATED HISTORY OF WEAPONS
RIFLES

Rupert Matthews

KINGSFORD EDITIONS

Contents

Introduction:
The Evolution of the Rifle

Ever since the first guns were invented in the 14th century there has been a drive to develop a gun that is light enough to be carried by a single person, but effective enough to be a reliable long-range tool on the battlefield and for hunting.

The earliest weapons light enough to be carried by a man were fairly inaccurate and hopelessly unreliable, especially in damp weather. They were invariably muzzle-loading guns and nearly all were smoothbore weapons. The mechanism for firing early guns was a key problem because they relied on a lit match or nearby fire. Once a mechanism, or lock, was invented that operated by striking a flint against steel to produce sparks, the gun was freed from the need to have a fire handy but was of little use in wet weather. It was the development of the percussion-cap in the early 19th

FLINTLOCK

A flintlock blunderbuss produced in India in about 1780, the attached whip shows that this was a weapon intended to be used from horseback. At this date the confused political scene in the Indian subcontinent enabled large bands of *dacoits*—mounted bandits—to operate freely. Some of these bands numbered over 5,000 men and were much feared by the smaller states, as well as by the people on whom they preyed. This weapon is typical of those carried by dacoits.

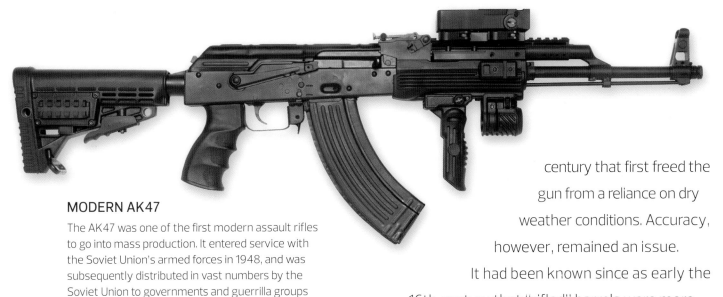

MODERN AK47

The AK47 was one of the first modern assault rifles to go into mass production. It entered service with the Soviet Union's armed forces in 1948, and was subsequently distributed in vast numbers by the Soviet Union to governments and guerrilla groups around the world. It has also been manufactured in other countries, both legally and illegally and has become one of the most numerous weapons in the modern world with an estimated 120 million having been made in a wide range of variants.

century that first freed the gun from a reliance on dry weather conditions. Accuracy, however, remained an issue.

It had been known since as early the 16th century that "rifled" barrels were more accurate than smoothbore barrels. Rifled weapons had helical grooves bored into the barrel that spun the bullet and stabilized its flight. However, the black gunpowder of the time produced residues that quickly fouled the rifling grooves and rendered such weapons inoperable.

Only in the late 19th century, with the development of smokeless powder, did it become possible to use rifled barrels time after time without difficulty. The new powder was also more powerful, making it possible to manufacture metal cartridges that combined bullet, powder, and percussion cap in one unit.

With all the elements of the modern rifle in place—rifled barrel, breech-loading mechanism, and metal cartridge—the 20th century saw a rapid development of the rifle as both a weapon of war and a tool for hunting. New polymers and metals were introduced to gun manufacture and innovations continued unabated, fueled by two devastating World Wars. Today, the rifle is more accurate, more reliable, and more effective than it has ever been. It remains the primary sidearm of the world's armies and is indispensable to hunters.

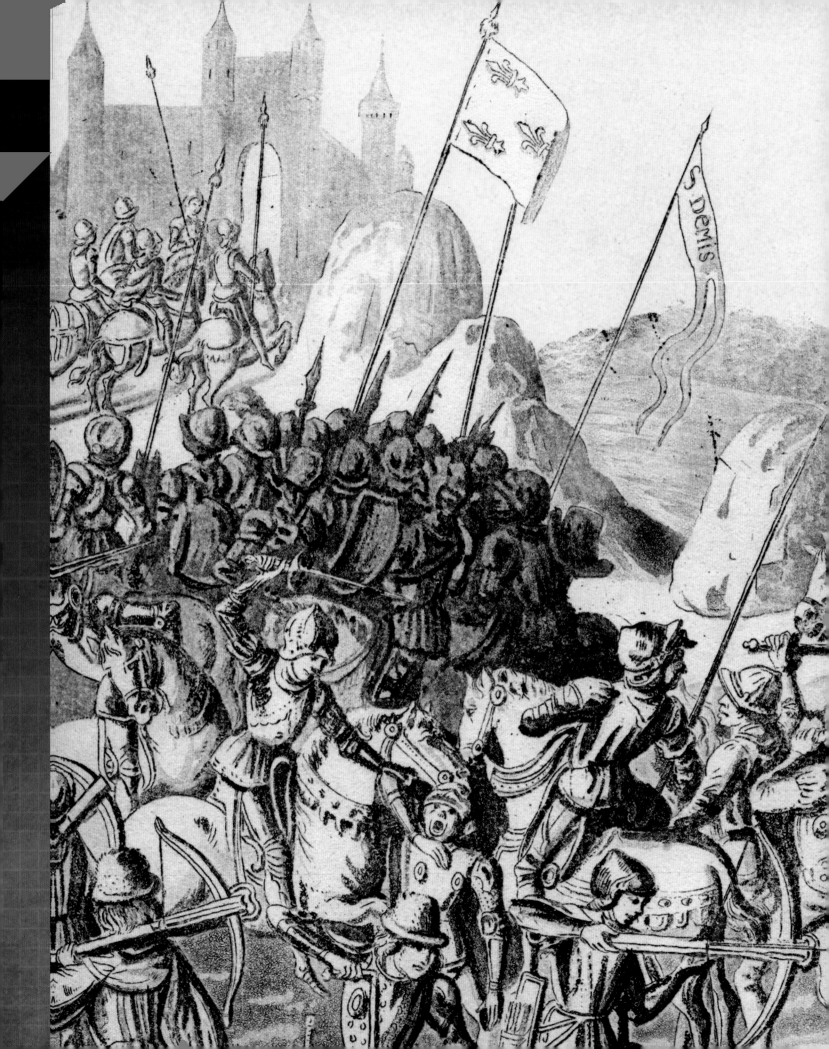

The First Firearms

A Revolution in Warfare

Guns revolutionized warfare in a way that no other weapon has ever done. Before the advent of guns all weapons depended in one way or another on muscle power. Swords, maces, and axes could make a mess of the human body at close range—the English double-handed axes at the Battle of Hastings shocked the Normans by their ability to kill a warhorse with a single blow—while arrows and javelins killed at longer ranges. But every weapon was limited by the strength of the man who wielded it. Firearms were different. Even the weakest man could pull a trigger. What mattered now was skill, determination, and firepower.

FOUGHT IN 1346 between King Edward III of England and King Philip VI of France, the Battle of Crecy is the first major battle in which guns were used. Contemporary chroniclers mention the guns only in passing (and they are not shown here), so it is thought that these weapons were of little importance on the field of battle. At this date the constituent parts of gunpowder had to be mixed just before it was used to ensure effective firing. A sudden, heavy shower of rain fell early in the battle and may well have dampened the gunpowder, effectively rendering the guns useless. Most casualties in the devastating English victory were inflicted by the massed use of longbows.

Early Guns

Gunpowder was invented in China sometime in the 9th century and remained the only known explosive for over a thousand years. The first known use of the explosive in a weapon was in about the year 1000 when a bamboo cane was used to shoot a spear using a charge of gunpowder. By about 1200, guns with metal barrels were being produced.

These fired balls and cylinders of stone or metal that more or less filled the bore of the barrel, greatly increasing the effectiveness of the weapons.

All these early guns were loaded from the barrel end. A touchhole at the closed end of the barrel allowed a hot coal or heated metal wire to set off the charge of gunpowder.

HAND GONNE

A French "hand gonne" made around 1400. The short barrel was attached to a wooden block with metal straps. Contemporary illustrations show men using these weapons in a variety of ways. Some were tucked under one arm, others were held over the shoulder.

The first effective tactic for the use of such inaccurate, short-range weapons in battle, developed by the Burgundians, had men with gonnes in the front rank of infantry formations mixed in with men holding pikes or other pole weapons. As the enemy closed to about 20 yards the gonnes were fired. The men with pole arms then stepped forward to cover the men with gonnes as they reloaded.

Wooden plank held by gunner

Iron strap holds barrel to plank

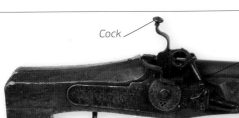

Lugs to fit into wooden handle

Four-clawed foot indicates noble ownership

CHINESE SIGNAL

A Chinese signal gun typical of those commonly made from the 12th–19th centuries. The bronze weapon has a pair of lugs to fix it to the wooden stock in which it was originally held. Bronze was favored for gun barrels as methods of casting iron were prone to create tiny flaws, which might cause the barrel to burst when fired. The dragon on the barrel has four claws on each foot, which marks this weapon out as part of a nobleman's arsenal.

Trigger may be pulled by hand, or wires in the holes can be attached to trip wires so that the gun fires when an enemy steps into the line of fire

Cock

Wheel-lock firing mechanism

Trigger has hole for string or wire

RAMPART GUN

A European rampart gun, or wall piece, made around 1600. The barrel was very long for the date in an effort to improve accuracy, so these guns were too heavy to be fired by one man. Instead, they were fired from the walls or ramparts of a fortification—with a string tied to the trigger if necessary. The barrel bore could be as much as one inch, throwing a heavy lead ball.

Matchlocks

As early as 1400 the traditional system of firing a gun—sticking a hot coal or wire into the touchhole—began to be seen as ineffective. The growth in numbers of guns on the battlefield—up to 600 handguns in a single Burgundian army in the 1420s—meant that keeping enough braziers going to heat the required number of wires was simply impractical. Instead each man was given a "match," a length of cord soaked in nitrates that would burn slowly and for prolonged periods. By 1440 a few handguns were equipped with a bent rod of metal that when pulled by the finger beneath the gun pushed the burning match into the touchhole on the top of the gun. This was the origin of the trigger and subsequently became known as the "matchlock."

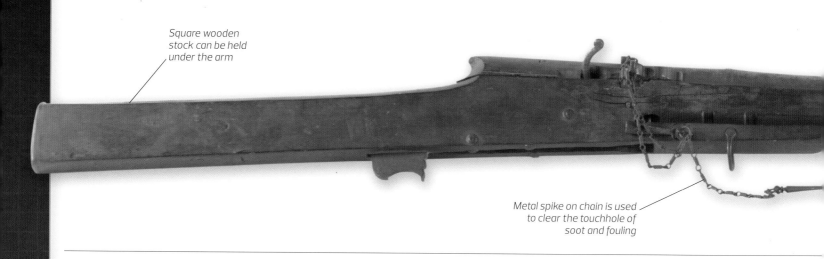

Square wooden stock can be held under the arm

Metal spike on chain is used to clear the touchhole of soot and fouling

CORNAC-GUN COMBINATION

In India, elephants were widely used in hunting and for transport. The mahout, or driver, had need of personal protection against bandits on the road, or against tigers when hunting. This 18th-century weapon combines the traditional mahout cornac, or goad, with a matchlock firearm. The hooked spike was used by the mahout to prod the elephant in the ear or on the forehead to give it commands—or as a punishment.

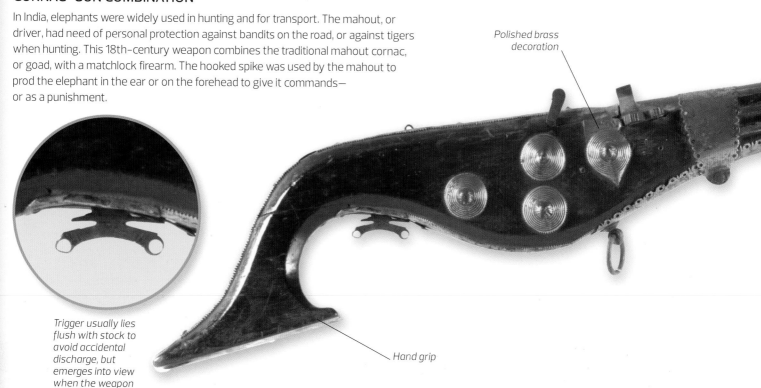

Polished brass decoration

Trigger usually lies flush with stock to avoid accidental discharge, but emerges into view when the weapon is cocked

Hand grip

MATCHLOCK CROSSBOW–GUN COMBINATION

This 16th-century weapon is a rare combination of a matchlock gun with a crossbow. The bow element is now missing but was originally mounted on the wooden stock near the muzzle of the gun barrel. The long slot in the wooden stock allowed the crossbow string and the short bolt that it shot (quarrel) to be hauled back and then held in position by the trigger. In this example the same trigger loosed the quarrel as fired the gun. Whether both weapons were shot at the same time is not known. It may be that the crossbow was a back up in case the matchlock failed for some reason, as early guns were wont to do.

Restraining lug for crossbow string

Original fixings for crossbow

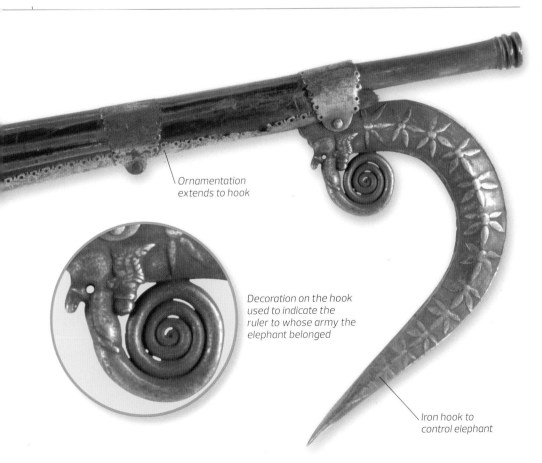

Ornamentation extends to hook

Decoration on the hook used to indicate the ruler to whose army the elephant belonged

Iron hook to control elephant

HERNAN CORTES

In 1519 the conquistador Hernan Cortes invaded and conquered the Aztec Empire in what is now Mexico. Although the Spaniards were outnumbered by about 40 to 1, they capitalized on the damaging effect that their matchlock firearms had on the stone-age Aztecs' morale as much as they used their actual ability to inflict casualties.

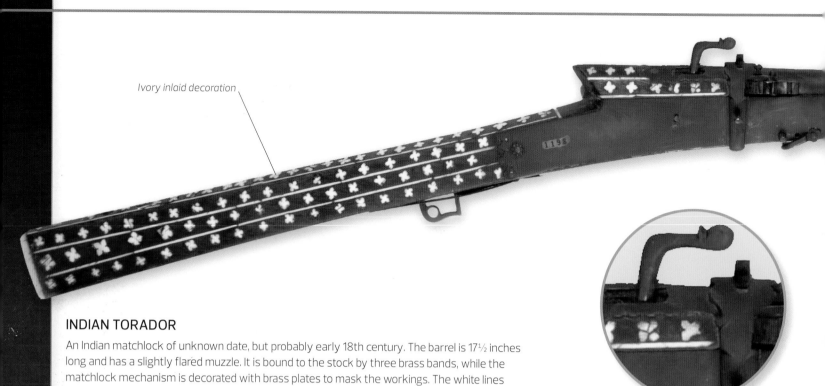

Ivory inlaid decoration

INDIAN TORADOR

An Indian matchlock of unknown date, but probably early 18th century. The barrel is 17½ inches long and has a slightly flared muzzle. It is bound to the stock by three brass bands, while the matchlock mechanism is decorated with brass plates to mask the workings. The white lines and stars are inlaid ivory, and the heel of the stock is covered with ivory. The high quality of decoration marks this out as a prestige weapon, which was clearly made for a rich client. The size of the weapon means that it was probably intended for a woman or older child and would have been used for hunting. Note the straight lines of the stock behind the trigger mechanism, a distinctive feature of weapons from the Indian subcontinent at this date.

Glowing match was held in this metal arm and lowered into the touch hole by the trigger. The length of match had to be constantly adjusted as it burned down

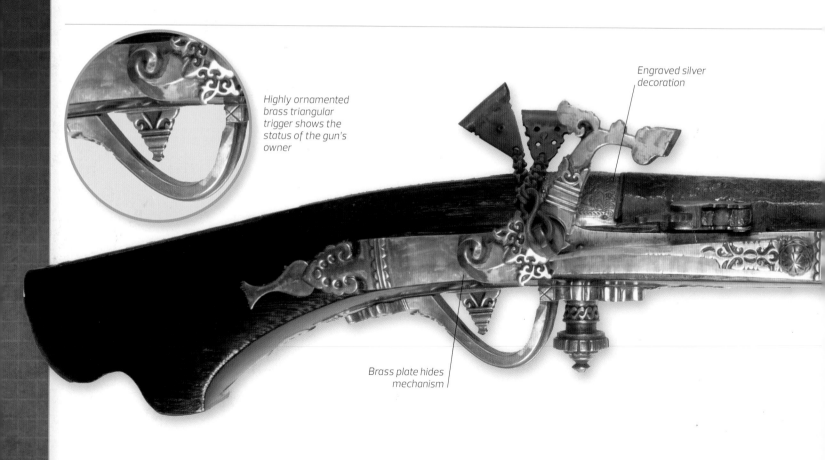

Highly ornamented brass triangular trigger shows the status of the gun's owner

Engraved silver decoration

Brass plate hides mechanism

Iron hoops hold barrel
to wooden stock

SHAH JAHAN OF DELHI

When Shah Jahan succeeded his father Jahangir as Mughal Emperor in 1628 he was able to field a vast army of 911,000 infantry, 185,000 cavalry and dozens of pieces of artillery. For ten years the army was kept occupied putting down rebellions, annexing border territories and imposing Mughal rule on India. Then in 1638 Shah Jahan attacked Persia. Shah Jahan himself heaped praise on his artillery and the gun founders of Jaigarh, but while these were instrumental in forcing the surrender of the great city of Kandahar, it was the musketeers who really made the difference. Armed with well made muskets, the infantry were well drilled and their officers had learned much from watching the Portuguese troops stationed at the trading post in Bengal. Supported by regular pay—a rarity in India at the time—the musketeers won a string of victories for Shah Jahan and his son Aurungzeb. Although a talented commander, Shah Jahan is today better known for the tomb he built for his wife—the Taj Mahal.

INDIAN MATCHLOCK RIFLE

This Indian matchlock rifle has a wooden body, cast-iron barrel, and highly ornate silver and brass decorations on the firing mechanism. It was made in the early 17th century.

Cast-iron barrel

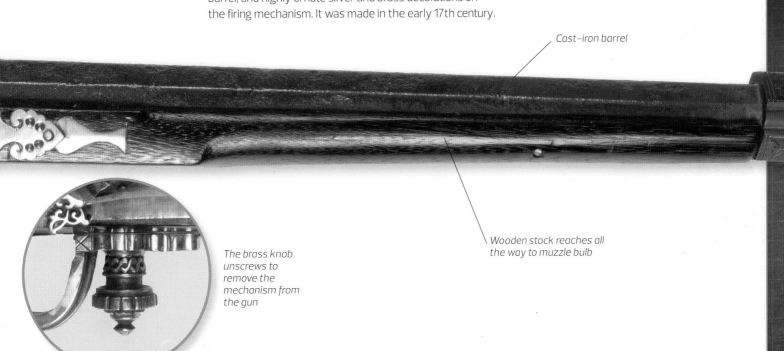

The brass knob
unscrews to
remove the
mechanism from
the gun

Wooden stock reaches all
the way to muzzle bulb

Wheel Locks

While the matchlock was simple and cheap, it had its drawbacks. The most crucial of these was that the match could easily go out if not properly attended to, especially in damp weather, leaving a soldier helpless. Even worse was the fact that the matches would often splutter and shed sparks. If a match did this when the soldier was close to exposed gunpowder the resulting blast could, and sometimes did, prove catastrophic. The solution to these problems, invented around 1500, was the wheel lock. The device proved to be more reliable, but was considerably more expensive. The very earliest wheel locks were pistols since the lack of a burning match meant the small guns could be safely tucked into holsters, boots or belts.

16TH-CENTURY WHEEL LOCK

A wheel-lock mechanism made in Britain in the 16th century. The weapon has two triggers and two firing mechanisms, as well as bone or ivory inlay around the muzzle. Short-barreled weapons such as this were extremely inaccurate and so were mostly for personal protection at short range. Note that the handle is almost directly in line with the barrel, which made the weapon easy to conceal, but resulted in an awkward grip when being fired.

Iron grips that originally held pieces of pyrites

Trigger guard stops triggers being pulled accidentally

GERMAN WHEEL-LOCK PISTOLS

A pair of heavy holster pistols made in Saxony, now part of Germany, in about 1590. The small key shown was used to wind up the spring that operated the wheel-lock mechanism. The matching box held cartridges—paper tubes containing a ball and a measured amount of gunpowder. To use such a cartridge, the firer bit the end off the cartridge that contained the ball and carefully poured the powder into the barrel. He then spat the ball down, following it with the scrunched-up paper. A metal rod then rammed the barrel contents into a densely packed mass, with the paper holding it all in position, ready to be fired. The thick, tear-resistant paper that was used survives today as the cartridge paper used by artists. Note the large globes at the butt end of the handle, which are made of timber and were sometimes weighted with lead. Loading a wheel lock was a time-consuming business, so once the pistol had been discharged, it could be held by the barrel and used as a club.

Heavy ball could be used as a club once the pistol was fired

WHEEL-LOCK MECHANISM C. 1730

This wheel-lock mechanism has several pieces. The upper "dog" section held a piece of pyrites (now missing) in its jaws. When the gun was ready to be fired, it was lowered to bring the pyrites into contact with the wheel (here hidden inside the mechanism). When the trigger was pulled, the wheel was released and driven round by a spring. As the toothed edges of the wheel rubbed on the pyrites, the resulting shower of sparks fell into the pan, which held a small amount of gunpowder. It ignited and the flash passed down the touchhole to set off the main charge and so fire the weapon.

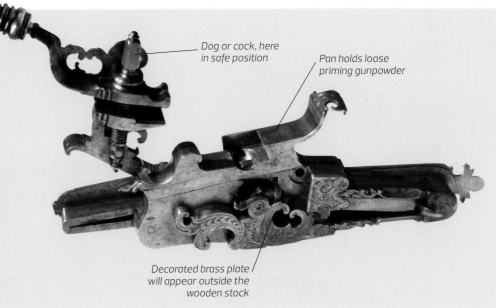

Dog or cock, here in safe position

Pan holds loose priming gunpowder

Decorated brass plate will appear outside the wooden stock

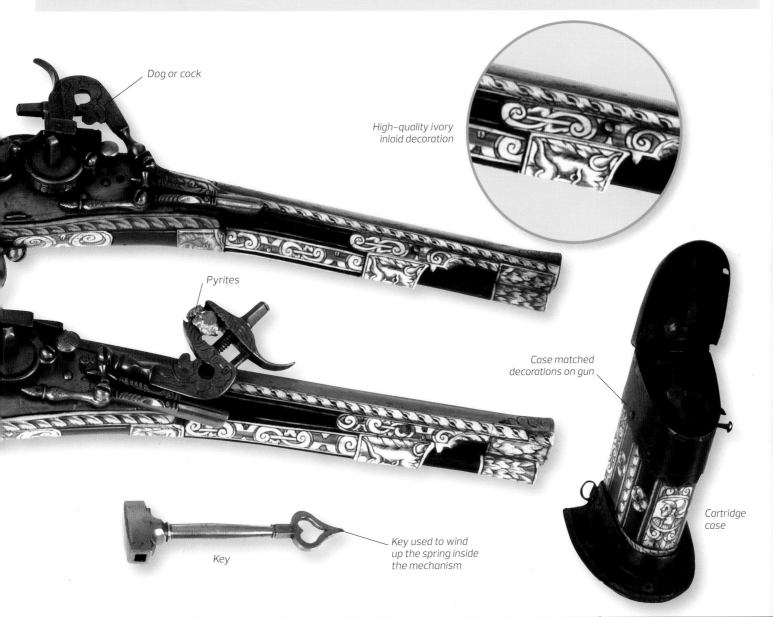

Dog or cock

High-quality ivory inlaid decoration

Pyrites

Case matched decorations on gun

Cartridge case

Key

Key used to wind up the spring inside the mechanism

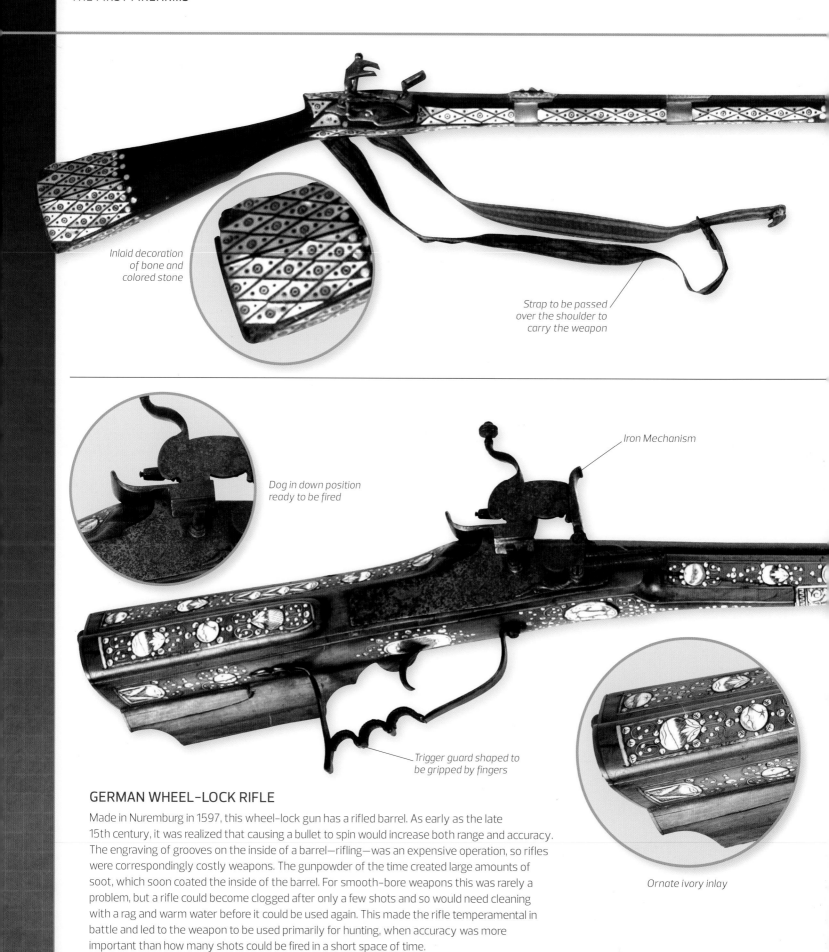

Inlaid decoration
of bone and
colored stone

Strap to be passed
over the shoulder to
carry the weapon

Dog in down position
ready to be fired

Iron Mechanism

Trigger guard shaped to
be gripped by fingers

Ornate ivory inlay

GERMAN WHEEL-LOCK RIFLE

Made in Nuremburg in 1597, this wheel-lock gun has a rifled barrel. As early as the late
15th century, it was realized that causing a bullet to spin would increase both range and accuracy.
The engraving of grooves on the inside of a barrel—rifling—was an expensive operation, so rifles
were correspondingly costly weapons. The gunpowder of the time created large amounts of
soot, which soon coated the inside of the barrel. For smooth-bore weapons this was rarely a
problem, but a rifle could become clogged after only a few shots and so would need cleaning
with a rag and warm water before it could be used again. This made the rifle temperamental in
battle and led to the weapon to be used primarily for hunting, when accuracy was more
important than how many shots could be fired in a short space of time.

Inlay continues along
wooden stock

GERMAN WHEEL-LOCK MUSKET

A German wheel-lock musket of the 17th century. The exceptionally long barrel was intended to increase accuracy, so this was probably a hunting weapon. The high-quality inlay work on the wooden stock and butt show that this was a weapon intended for the luxury market. The terminology of these early hand weapons can be confusing. Generally, a musket was a gun that was so long or heavy that the barrel was rested on a forked stick to be fired. An arquebus was a slightly smaller weapon that could be fired without the stick rest. A caliver was an even lighter weapon, often with a short barrel. However, all these terms could be used to refer to each type of weapon, so making sense of battle reports is not always easy.

Barrel extends beyond ornamented wooden stock. Soot and other residue left by the large volume of smoke created by the discharge of black powder forms around the metal muzzle where it can be easily cleaned off

Wooden ramrod

Wooden ramrod held under
the barrel by bone loops

TERCIO TACTICAL DEPLOYMENT

In the early 16th century, the Spanish army developed a tactical deployment, the *tercio*, that would dominate European warfare for a century. The *tercio* was composed of three groups of infantry: armored pikemen, men with firearms and men armed with swords and shields. The usual formation was for the pikemen to form a hollow square, which was proof against cavalry. When horsemen threatened the others would shelter inside the square, but at other times would deploy outside. The men with guns were used to fire at enemy troops. If the enemy formation was disrupted or appeared weak the swordsmen would launch an assault. Neither group of men would move very far from the safety provided by the armored pikemen. The *tercio* ruled supreme until improvements in weapons technology rendered the pikemen redundant.

The Musket Comes of Age

By the year 1700 the musket had become the standard infantry weapon in all European armies. The dominance of the musket came about due to technological and tactical developments. Improvements to methods of making gunpowder, combined with the flintlock mechanism made firearms much more reliable, rendering edged weapons far less effective than they had been. The development of the bayonet enabled musket-armed men to fend off cavalry attacks for the first time.

Alongside these improvements to the weapon, the adoption of the line as the standard infantry formation allowed most, if not all, of the men to fire their muskets at the same time. This line formation created a volley of much-greater hitting power than earlier formations had achieved. The effect of massed firepower overcame the inherent inaccuracy of the musket and made speed of loading a prime consideration in battle.

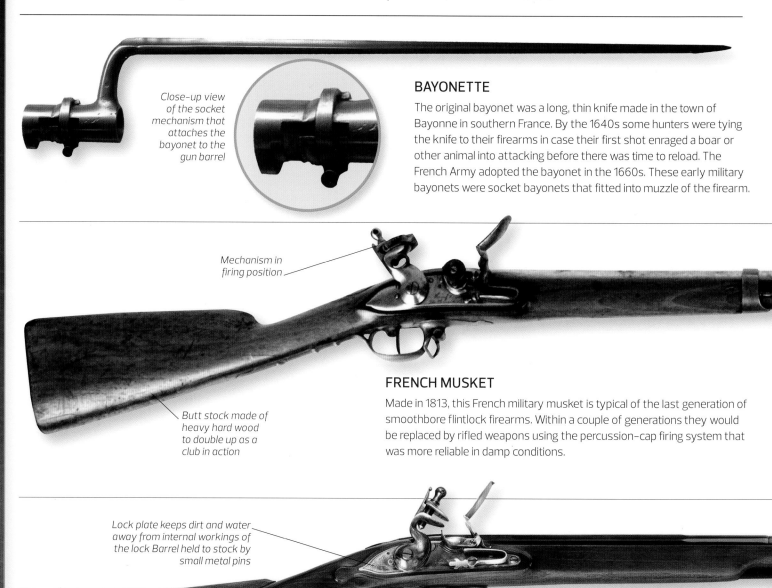

Close-up view of the socket mechanism that attaches the bayonet to the gun barrel

BAYONETTE

The original bayonet was a long, thin knife made in the town of Bayonne in southern France. By the 1640s some hunters were tying the knife to their firearms in case their first shot enraged a boar or other animal into attacking before there was time to reload. The French Army adopted the bayonet in the 1660s. These early military bayonets were socket bayonets that fitted into muzzle of the firearm.

Mechanism in firing position

Butt stock made of heavy hard wood to double up as a club in action

FRENCH MUSKET

Made in 1813, this French military musket is typical of the last generation of smoothbore flintlock firearms. Within a couple of generations they would be replaced by rifled weapons using the percussion-cap firing system that was more reliable in damp conditions.

Lock plate keeps dirt and water away from internal workings of the lock Barrel held to stock by small metal pins

The flint is missing from this weapon. In fact flints were relatively rare in the interior of North America, so the importation of replacement flints, carefully knapped to produce a strong spark, was an important trade

FLINTLOCK MECHANISM

The flintlock mechanism was invented around 1610 and proved to be both cheaper and more reliable than its predecessors. The mechanism consisted of three parts. The cock was a metal arm that held a flint gripped in a small vice. The cock was attached to a spring that snapped it forward when the trigger was pulled. The pan was a small metal tray on to which was placed a small amount of gunpowder. The frizzen was an L-shaped piece of steel. The lower part was placed over the pan to keep the powder in position while the upright part pointed upward. When the trigger was pulled the cock would move rapidly forward to strike the frizzen. As the flint scraped along the frizzen it created sparks, while at the same time pushing the frizzen forward and exposing the powder in the pan. The sparks ignited the powder which then flashed through the touchhole to ignite the main charge and fire the weapon.

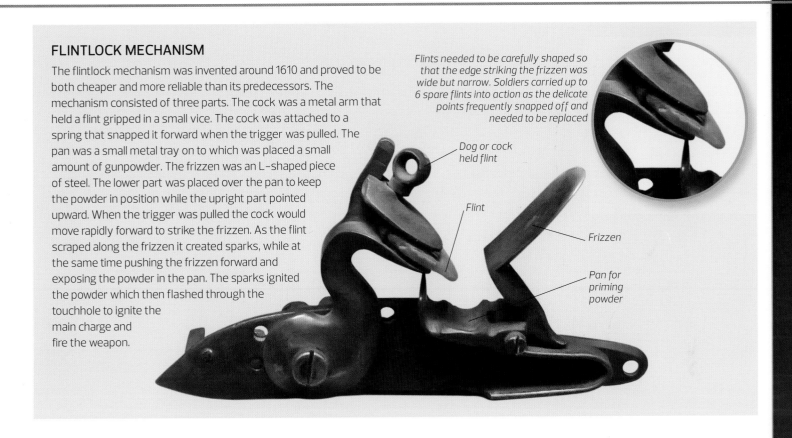

Flints needed to be carefully shaped so that the edge striking the frizzen was wide but narrow. Soldiers carried up to 6 spare flints into action as the delicate points frequently snapped off and needed to be replaced

Dog or cock held flint

Flint

Frizzen

Pan for priming powder

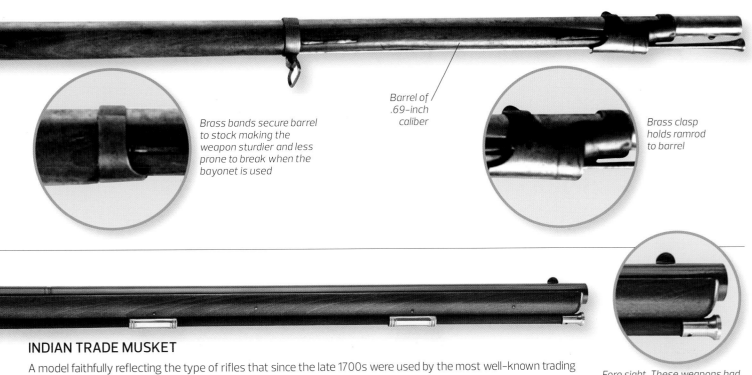

Brass bands secure barrel to stock making the weapon sturdier and less prone to break when the bayonet is used

Barrel of .69-inch caliber

Brass clasp holds ramrod to barrel

Fore sight. These weapons had a rudimentary fore sight as this was considered to be a desirable feature by frontiersmen, though in fact the guns were no more accurate than military muskets which lacked them

INDIAN TRADE MUSKET

A model faithfully reflecting the type of rifles that since the late 1700s were used by the most well-known trading companies (Northwest Co., Hudson's Bay Co., American Fur Co.) for the trades with Native Americans and white hunters. The finish and fit was not carefully crafted in consideration of the rough use these guns would receive, but they have the classical lines of the old European muskets produced both by European manufacturers and the most well-known American manufacturers, such as Leman, Henry, Tryon, and Deringer. The wooden ramrod and large trigger guard were typical features of these guns.

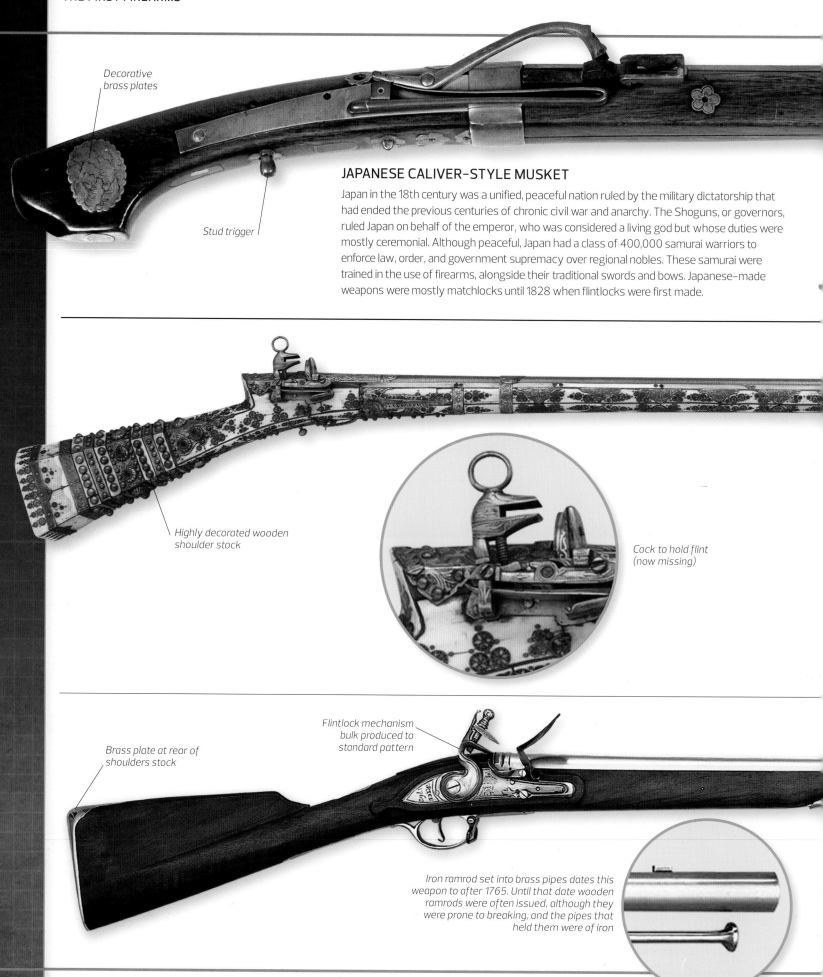

Decorative brass plates

Stud trigger

JAPANESE CALIVER-STYLE MUSKET

Japan in the 18th century was a unified, peaceful nation ruled by the military dictatorship that had ended the previous centuries of chronic civil war and anarchy. The Shoguns, or governors, ruled Japan on behalf of the emperor, who was considered a living god but whose duties were mostly ceremonial. Although peaceful, Japan had a class of 400,000 samurai warriors to enforce law, order, and government supremacy over regional nobles. These samurai were trained in the use of firearms, alongside their traditional swords and bows. Japanese-made weapons were mostly matchlocks until 1828 when flintlocks were first made.

Highly decorated wooden shoulder stock

Cock to hold flint (now missing)

Flintlock mechanism bulk produced to standard pattern

Brass plate at rear of shoulders stock

Iron ramrod set into brass pipes dates this weapon to after 1765. Until that date wooden ramrods were often issued, although they were prone to breaking, and the pipes that held them were of iron

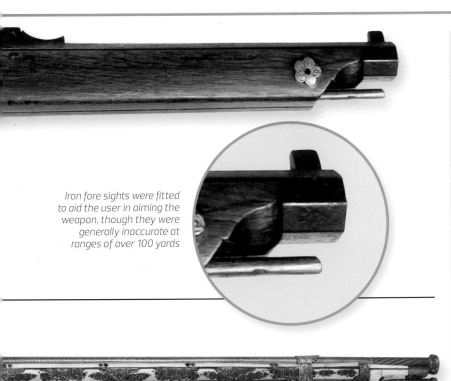

Iron fore sights were fitted to aid the user in aiming the weapon, though they were generally inaccurate at ranges of over 100 yards

THE BATTLE OF FONTENOY

At the Battle of Fontenoy in 1745 the veteran French Grenadier Guards advanced on the equally steady British First Guards. When the two lines were only 40 yards apart the French halted. Lord Charles Hay of the British stepped forward and invited the French to fire first. Comte d'Auteroche of the French shouted back "No, you fire first."

This bizarre event took place because muskets had a range of under 100 yards but were most effective at 25 yards, moreover the first volley was deemed to be the most successful since the weapons had been loaded at leisure and with care. The temptation was to open fire as soon as the enemy got within range rather than to wait until they were closer. In practice, only well-trained veterans could be relied upon to stand still until the enemy were as close as 25 yards before opening fire, so most musketry took place at longer ranges.

At Fontenoy, both sides wanted the other to shoot first, so that they could then dash forward and deliver a crushing volley before the other had time to reload. In the event, Auteroche then saw the British Third Guards advancing at the trot to attack his flank, so the French fired first and then began a fighting retreat. The French won the day.

TURKISH FLINTLOCK

A Turkish weapon from the 18th century. The relatively short, wide-bore barrel is fixed to the stock by metal bands. The Ottoman Empire was then at its greatest extent, covering all of North Africa plus much of the Middle East and the Balkans. A series of short wars against Russia, however, had shown the Turkish military to be old fashioned and ineptly run. Reform efforts by Selim III and Mahmud I involved the importation to Turkey of modern firearms, such as this, and of craftsmen to make them, but these efforts were blocked by vested interests in the military who believed their status and power to be threatened by the reforms.

Metal ramrod

BROWN BESS

In 1722 the British Army introduced a new form of musket known officially as the Long Land Pattern Musket, but soon dubbed the Brown Bess by the men. The Brown Bess remained the primary infantry weapon of the British until 1838. The origins of the nickname are obscure, but British soldiers were already calling their guns "Bess," perhaps from the Dutch "buss" for barrel. The "Brown" element may have been a reference to a chemical treatment given to the barrels to stop them rusting. The musket had a bore of 0.75 inch, a barrel length of 46 inches and weighed 10 pounds. It proved to be a hardy, reliable weapon that performed well in the tough conditions of campaigning. Later versions of this gun included a cavalry carbine with a 26-inch barrel, a naval version with a 37-inch barrel, and the India Pattern, made for the East India Company, which had a 39-inch barrel and a lighter construction.

Blunderbusses

Throughout most of the history of the gun there have been effectively no restrictions on the private ownership or use of firearms. Firearms often featured in robberies, both in the hands of the criminal and of their intended victims. Robbers tended to prefer weapons that could be hidden easily, and so mostly used pistols. Those likely to be attacked had good reason to keep their weapons on display and preferred weapons guaranteed to inflict maximum damage at short ranges, so it was that the blunderbuss came to be their weapon of choice. With its characteristic flared muzzle, the blunderbuss fired lead shot over a wide area and was deadly at short range. Private security guards at banks, the homes of the rich and elsewhere were routinely armed with blunderbuss and sabre.

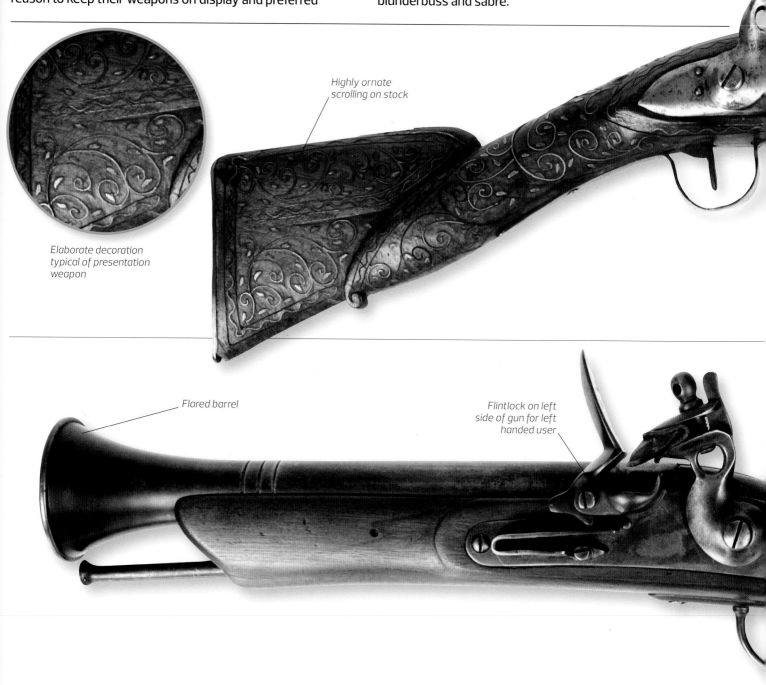

Highly ornate scrolling on stock

Elaborate decoration typical of presentation weapon

Flared barrel

Flintlock on left side of gun for left handed user

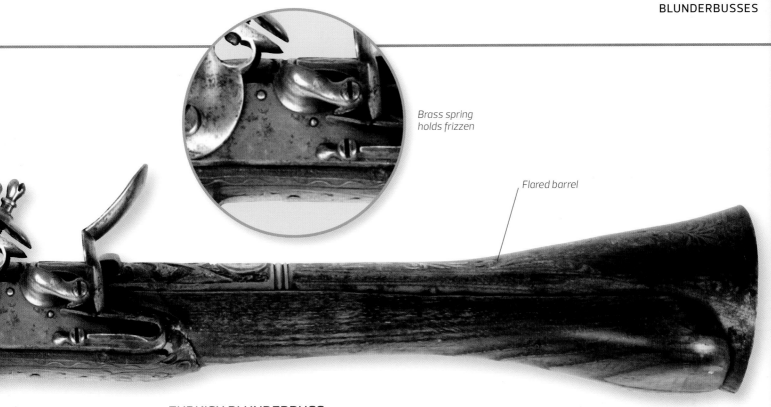

Brass spring holds frizzen

Flared barrel

TURKISH BLUNDERBUSS

This ornate blunderbuss was given to the French general Aimabale Pélissier by his wife while they were living in Oran, then a French colony, during the 1840s. The workmanship is Turkish and the gun has elaborate carving on the wooden parts as well as a high-quality mechanism. Pélissier is thought to have been carrying this murderous short-range weapon when he commanded the French infantry at the Battle of Malakoff in the Crimean War. The victory he won effectively decided the war, and a grateful Emperor Napoleon III created him Duc de Malakoff.

AMERICAN BLUNDERBUSS

This blunderbuss was made at the Harpers Ferry Armory, official manufacturing center of weapons for the US Government. It was probably made in the 1810s for naval use. During those days of wooden warships a battle between ships was sometimes decided when the crew of one ship boarded the other. In the conditions where large numbers of men were confined on cramped decks, a blunderbuss would have made an awesomely effective weapon.

Flint in firing position

Short shoulder stock

EUROPEAN SHORT BLUNDERBUSS

This short-barreled blunderbuss carries no marks, but its style indicates it was made somewhere in Europe during the early 20th century. Part of the effectiveness of a blunderbuss for personal protection lay in the flared mouth of the barrel. In itself this only marginally expanded the scatter pattern of the shot as it was fired, but it did mean that a would-be assailant was presented with an intimidatingly wide muzzle. This short-barreled weapon could be hidden beneath a coat or cloak and whipped out in dramatic fashion when needed.

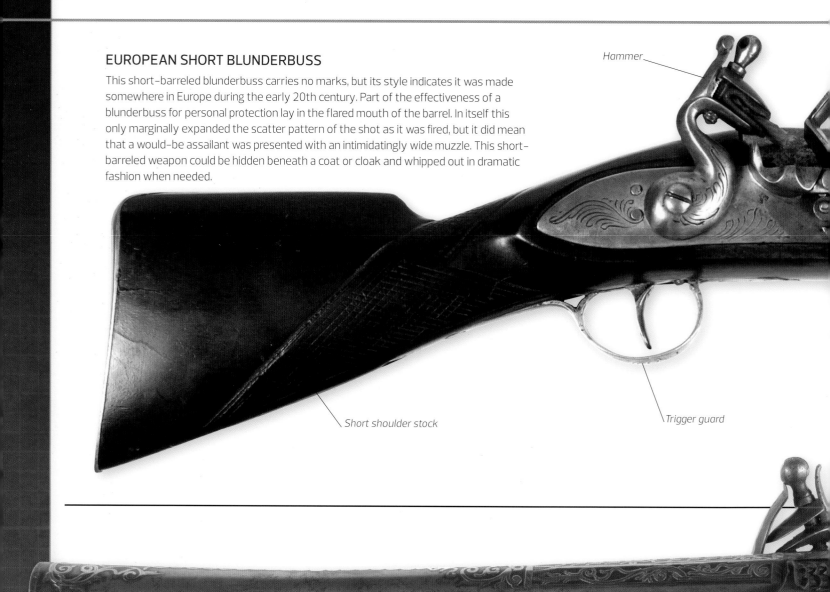

Hammer

Short shoulder stock

Trigger guard

CAUCASIAN MOUNTAINEER

Although this weapon looks like a pistol, it is in fact a form of blunderbuss. The weapon is designed to fire shot, not a single bullet or ball. This example has elegant carving on the wood and silver decorative plates. It is thought to have been used by a bandit in the Caucasian Mountains during the early 19th century.

Decorative metal plates hold the mechanism in place within the stock

Wide muzzle intended to look intimidating

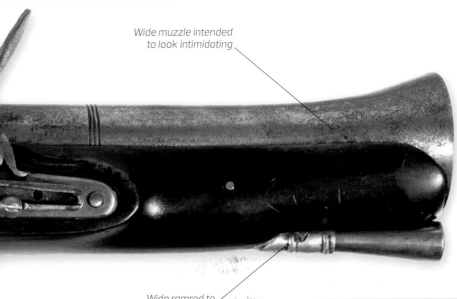

The cast hammer and nipple were the weak point of this design as rain or dew could enter the nipple and render the weapon likely to misfire

Wide ramrod to match barrel base

STAND AND DELIVER

The confrontation between pistol and blunderbuss was epitomized in the actions of highwaymen and coach guards during the 18th century when long-distance coach travel by road was comparatively common. The majority of robbers used heavy holster pistols that had long barrels and fired a ball almost as heavy as that of a musket. These weapons were useful in a wide variety of situations and were relatively accurate for their day. Guards preferred the blunderbuss with its awesome blast at short range and the lack of a need to aim carefully to injure the highwayman. In practice the winner was usually the man who got his gun into action first.

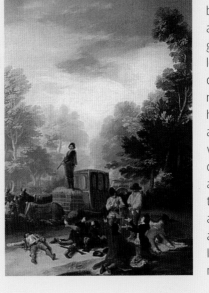

Carving on wooden stock is typical of the Caucasian region

Trap Guns

Trap guns were mainly designed for hunting. A screw bolt or similar mechanism was used to attach the gun firmly in position to a tree or post. The barrel was then loaded and set so that it aimed at the piece of bait. The bait was then connected with wire to the trigger. When an animal moved the bait, the chain would pull the trigger and fire the gun. The flared mouth of the weapon ensured a good spread of shot, with the aim of crippling the animal. The hunter, hearing the gun go off, would then approach to finish the kill. With indoor traps intended for human targets, guns such as the Danish trap gun shown here were typically wired to a door and fired when the door was opened.

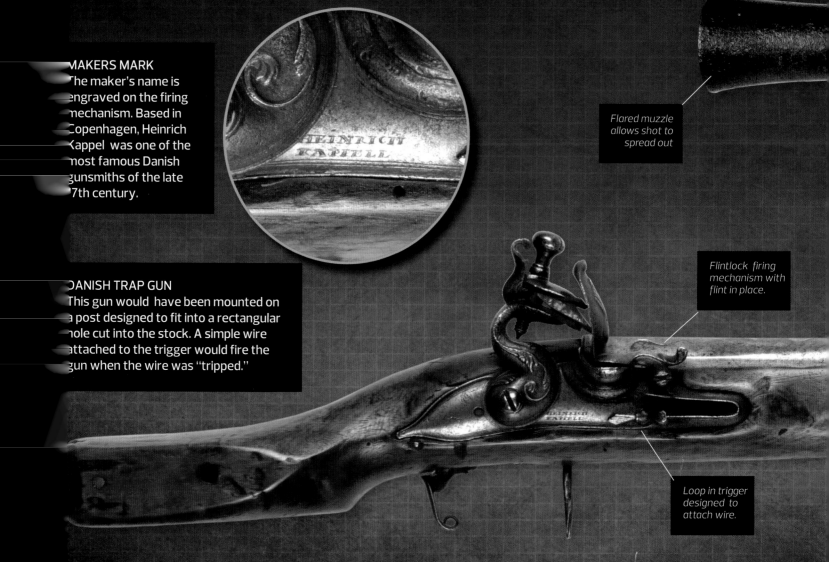

MAKERS MARK
The maker's name is engraved on the firing mechanism. Based in Copenhagen, Heinrich Kappel was one of the most famous Danish gunsmiths of the late 17th century.

DANISH TRAP GUN
This gun would have been mounted on a post designed to fit into a rectangular hole cut into the stock. A simple wire attached to the trigger would fire the gun when the wire was "tripped."

Flared muzzle allows shot to spread out

Flintlock firing mechanism with flint in place.

Loop in trigger designed to attach wire.

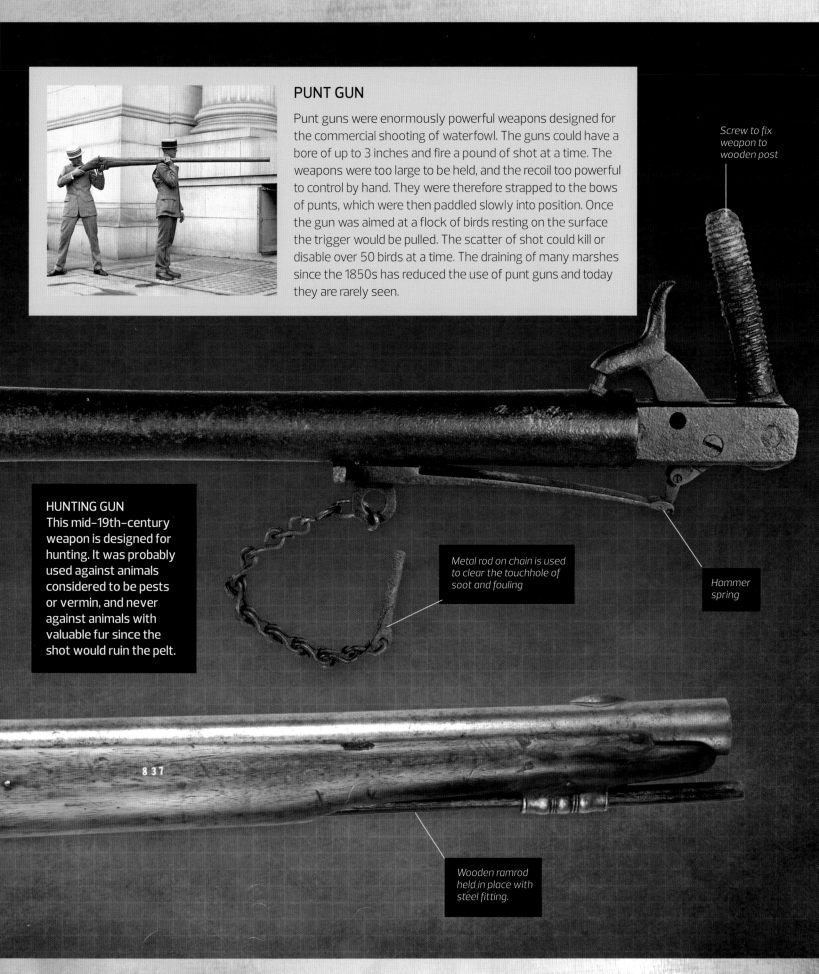

PUNT GUN

Punt guns were enormously powerful weapons designed for the commercial shooting of waterfowl. The guns could have a bore of up to 3 inches and fire a pound of shot at a time. The weapons were too large to be held, and the recoil too powerful to control by hand. They were therefore strapped to the bows of punts, which were then paddled slowly into position. Once the gun was aimed at a flock of birds resting on the surface the trigger would be pulled. The scatter of shot could kill or disable over 50 birds at a time. The draining of many marshes since the 1850s has reduced the use of punt guns and today they are rarely seen.

Screw to fix weapon to wooden post

HUNTING GUN
This mid-19th-century weapon is designed for hunting. It was probably used against animals considered to be pests or vermin, and never against animals with valuable fur since the shot would ruin the pelt.

Metal rod on chain is used to clear the touchhole of soot and fouling

Hammer spring

8 37

Wooden ramrod held in place with steel fitting.

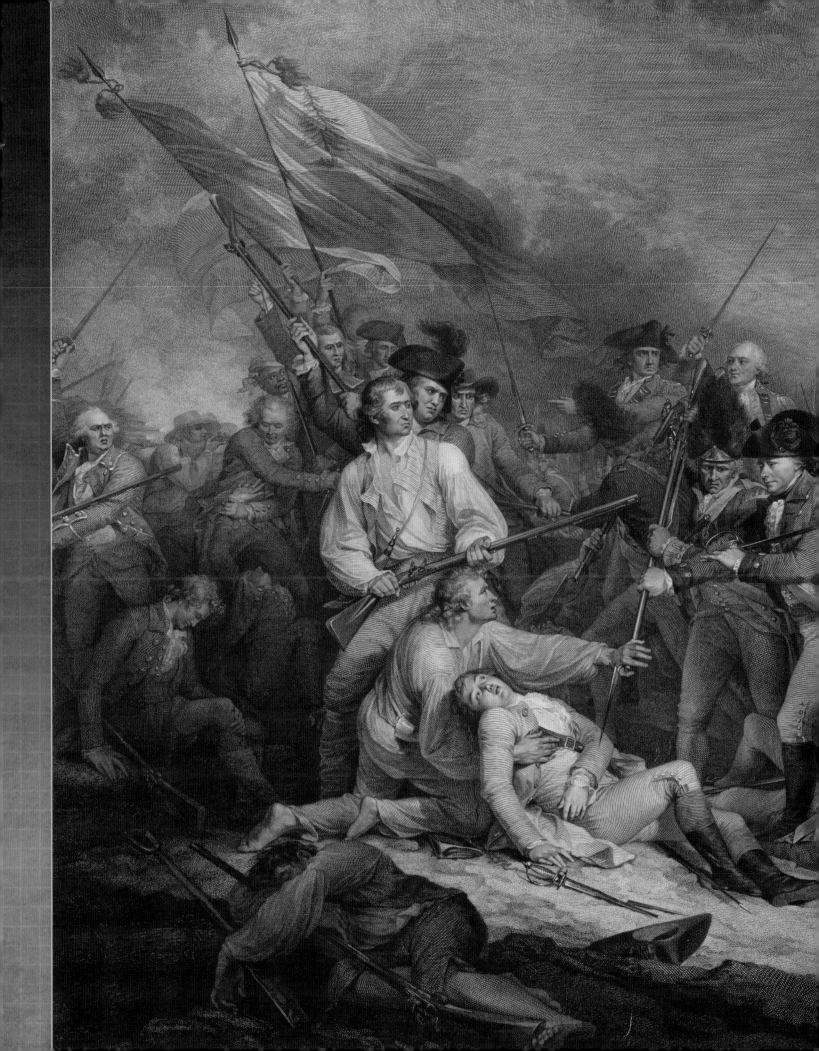

The Revolutionary Wars

The Age of Enlightenment

What history knows as the Revolutionary Wars came at a critical time for firearms. Inspired by the revolutionary ideals of the philosophical Enlightenment, and by very practical matters of taxation and democracy, 13 of the British colonies in America declared themselves independent. The resulting war with Britain led indirectly to the much larger and more devastating French Revolutionary Wars that saw the Emperor Napoleon rise and fall from power as wars raged over Europe from 1792 to 1815. For the previous century firearms technology had been almost static, with the flintlock dominating. The pressure of global warfare on a massive scale, however, forced men to innovate. Rifles entered military service, muskets were employed in new tactics, and a number of experimental weapons were produced. The Revolutionary Wars led to an unprecedented revolution in weaponry.

BUNKER HILL: The Battle of Bunker Hill on June 17, 1775, was primarily fought with muskets at ranges of under 100 paces. During the final British assault, the colonial forces ran out of ammunition and, lacking bayonets, were reduced to using their musket butts as clubs.

A Revolution in Warfare

The war that split the 13 American Colonies from Britain raged for more than eight years in the late 18th century and was extended by the interventions of three great maritime powers: France, Spain, and the Netherlands. The conflict grew out of complex social and political movements that combined a growing self identity in the colonies with powerful ideas of human rights. On the field of battle the war showed that the traditional methods of waging war in Europe were not only unsuited to the very different physical terrain in North America, but were also increasingly outmoded as weapons technology evolved. In particular the use of rifles and skirmishing tactics by light infantry showed the way to the future.

NOCK VOLLEY GUN

A Nock volley gun dating to around 1790. This awesome weapon has seven barrels welded together, all discharged simultaneously by a single flintlock trigger. It was designed for naval use, the idea being that a man armed with a volley gun would wait in the rigging until an enemy ship came alongside and then fire his weapon down on to the crowded enemy decks. The chief drawback was that gun was so heavy and had such an awesome recoil that only an especially strong man could use it. Moreover, the time it took to reload all the barrels meant it was slow to use. The weapon has become well known in recent years through its use by the fictional Sergeant Harper in the *Sharpe* series of novels.

The standard flintlock mechanism sent a flash from the powder pan through a vent to the central barrel, which then fired. As the central barrel fired, the flash traveled through vents to the other barrels which then fired simultaneously.

Multiple barrels

Lock plate

Butt stock

Ramrod

The Nock had seven barrels that were welded together along their length. The central barrel was surrounded by six more.

The American Revolution

During the American Revolutionary War the British suffered badly at the hands of local Americans, who adopted skirmishing tactics. While the British marched in massed formations that were suited to open battlefields and to set–piece battles between large armies, the Americans adopted looser tactics. Notably these involved men working alone or in pairs, shooting at long range from behind trees or rocks. These snipers inflicted relatively few casualties, but their main importance was that they harassed and worried the men while disrupting their tight formations before a battle began in earnest. It wasn't long before all armies were training teams of men for skirmishing tactics and adopting suitable weaponry. By the early 1800s the British were themselves experimenting with rifles that until then had been confined to hunting.

THE MARCH TO LEXINGTON

On the fateful night of April 18, 1775, 700 British troops left Boston, Massachusetts, with orders to seize weapons and supplies that belonged to the local militia at nearby Lexington and Concord. Although the political situation in Britain's North American colonies was fractious, both sides hoped the situation could be resolved peacefully. It was not to be.

The British authorities feared that the local militia might use their weapons if the dispute turned violent. When the British reached Lexington, they found 77 men of the local militia drawn up on the village green. Major John Pitcairn led 400 men to confront the militia and shouted an order to lay down their weapons and disperse.

At this tense moment a shot was fired, though it has never been agreed by whom. The British believed they were under attack and fired a succession of volleys and charged with the bayonet. Eight militiamen were killed, and the American Revolutionary War had begun.

KENTUCKY RIFLES

Rifled barrels, those with internal spiral grooves to spin the ball, had been manufactured in Europe since the 16th century. The spin gave the ball greater stability in flight, increasing both range and accuracy. The need for the ball to have a snug fit in the grooves made these weapons slow to load, while the gunpowder of the time left a sooty deposit that soon clogged the rifling and made it unusable. As a consequence rifles were used for hunting, where a single accurate shot was important, but were avoided by the military, who preferred a less–accurate gun that could be fire rapidly without jamming. In North America immigrant German gunsmiths adapted the basic European rifle by increasing the length of the barrel from 30 inches to 46. This massively increased the accuracy of the gun, but made it even slower to reload and more prone to fouling.

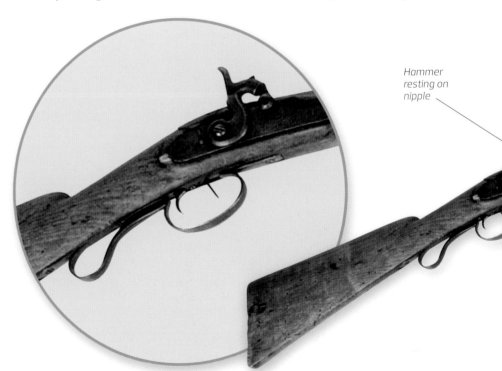

Hammer resting on nipple

Double-set triggers were developed for hunting, and were much safer than the conventional hair trigger, which will fire with a slight pull. Pulling the first trigger "sets" the firing mechanism to hair-trigger mode, after which the second trigger is pulled to fire the weapon.

LIGHT-HORSE HARRY LEE

Henry Lee was a Virginian lawyer and politician who found fame as a cavalry commander in the American Revolutionary Wars. He began his military career as a captain in the Virginia Dragoons, but was soon commanding an informal body of men dubbed "Lee's Legion," made up of troops specially trained and equipped for irregular warfare. With this body of cavalry he roamed the more remote areas of the war zone, raiding British outposts and supply routes. By 1781 Lee and his men were more closely attached to the main Patriot armies. He fought at the battles of Guilford Courthouse and Eutaw Springs, and was present when the British commander Cornwallis surrendered at Yorktown. Throughout this time Lee made good use of firearms, particularly in the ambush that came to be known as Pyle's Massacre, where his men killed 93 Loyalists with no loss to themselves. Lee was the father of the rather more famous Robert E. Lee of the US Civil War.

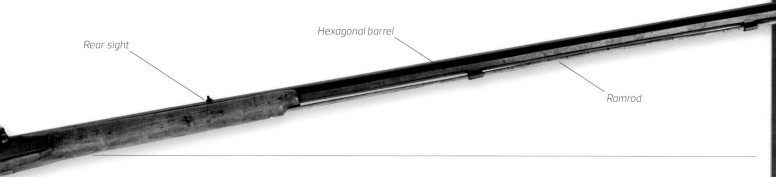

Rear sight

Hexagonal barrel

Ramrod

LONG RIFLE

Although the American Long Rifle was primarily a hunting weapon, the recruitment of frontiersmen into the early US army brought this weapon into military use. The early US Army was short of weapons and recruits were encouraged to bring their own whenever possible. In 1815 General Andrew Jackson defeated the British at the Battle of New Orleans. About a quarter of Jackson's army were riflemen from Kentucky, giving rise to the song "Hunters of Kentucky," in which the advantages of the "Kentucky rifle" were emphasized. Thereafter the long rifle was often called the Kentucky rifle, though only a minority of them came from that state.

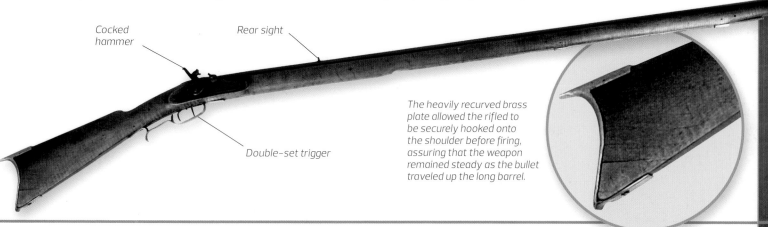

Cocked hammer

Rear sight

Double-set trigger

The heavily recurved brass plate allowed the rifled to be securely hooked onto the shoulder before firing, assuring that the weapon remained steady as the bullet traveled up the long barrel.

Craft Rifles

Before the mass-production techniques of the industrial revolution, all guns were made individually by hand. The intricacies of making the moving parts of the lock were challenging, but the processes involved in making the smooth, precision rifling on the inside of a barrel were always especially difficult. Mass production enabled greater quantities of good-quality weapons to be made at low cost, but they could never match the superior quality of the skilled craftsmen. To this day, craft companies such as Proctor or Holland & Holland custom-make weapons to suit individual customers. Elsewhere, local gunsmiths continue to turn out weapons of varying quality, some of which are copies of factory-made models. The Khyber Pass region of Pakistan is particularly noted for this trade.

CAMEL RIFLE
This rifle was collected during the First World War in Arabia, where it was used by a traditional tribal warrior mounted on a camel. The elaborate decoration is typical of Arab weapons of this date and need not mark this out as belonging to a high-status individual. At this date camel-mounted Arabs carried swords as well as these very long rifles. The long barrel was intended to increase accuracy, while the additional weight was acceptable due to the carrying capacity of the camel.

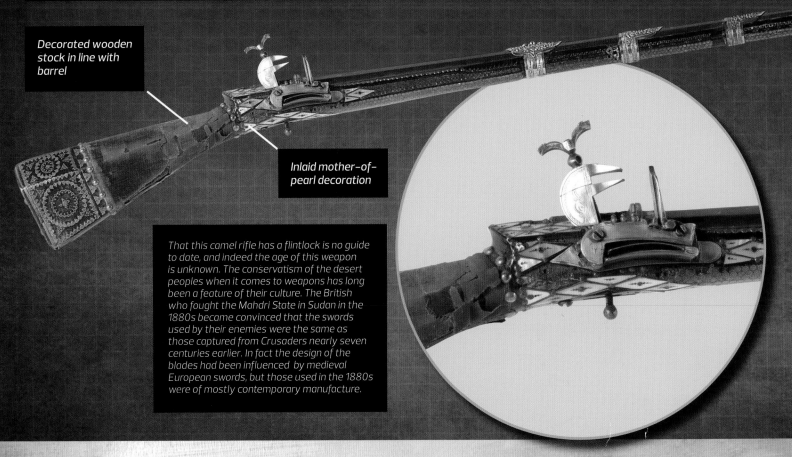

Decorated wooden stock in line with barrel

Inlaid mother-of-pearl decoration

That this camel rifle has a flintlock is no guide to date, and indeed the age of this weapon is unknown. The conservatism of the desert peoples when it comes to weapons has long been a feature of their culture. The British who fought the Mahdri State in Sudan in the 1880s became convinced that the swords used by their enemies were the same as those captured from Crusaders nearly seven centuries earlier. In fact the design of the blades had been influenced by medieval European swords, but those used in the 1880s were of mostly contemporary manufacture.

Heavy wood stock
with long barrel

19TH-CENTURY CRAFT RIFLE

This heavy weapon is typical of the rifles used by camel riders in Arabia and
North Africa for much of the 18th and 19th centuries. It is robustly made with
the stout wooden stock extending all the way to the muzzle of the barrel. The
guns tended to get bounced around a lot as the camels trotted over the rough,
broken ground of the deserts, so the construction needed to be strong enough
to withstand such treatment. The flintlock mechanism continued in use in
desert countries long after it fell out of favor elsewhere. There was little danger
of the gunpowder becoming damp in the desert.

*Close-up view of the flintlock mechanism. Unlike
in temperate zones there was no danger of guns
misfiring in wet weather, so a key advantage of
the percussion cap was irrelevant.*

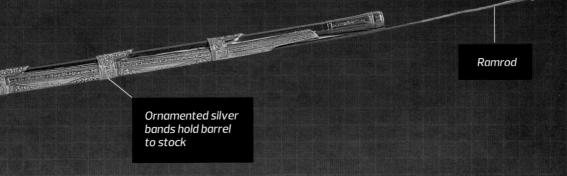

Ramrod

Ornamented silver
bands hold barrel
to stock

KHYBER PASS COPY FIREARM

Craftsmen in Pakistan villages around the Khyber Pass are famous for producing handmade copies of rifles and other weapons
of all kinds. Some of the better examples are almost indistinguishable from the originals and can be just as reliable and effective.
However, a lack of high quality steel can make some Khyber Pass copies liable to misfire, burst, or otherwise be ineffective. This
example is a copy of a 19th-century Martini carbine.

Receiver on copies
often engraved with
inaccurate writing

Barrels are handmade
and of greatly varying
quality

The Napoleonic Wars

When King Louis XVI of France was executed in the course of the French Revolution the other monarchies of Europe moved to stop the movement spreading. The wars that followed lasted for 22 years and came to be dominated by a French general named Napoleon Bonaparte, who used his military skills to become Emperor of the French and eventually to rule most of Europe.

One country consistently stood out against him and was almost continuously at war with France for a generation: Great Britain. From 1808 to 1815 the land element of the war was concentrated in the Iberian Peninsula, where Britain helped the Portuguese and Spanish throw off French rule. This Peninsular War saw the entrance into European warfare of weapons and tactics developed in the American Revolutionary War.

DRUMMER-BOY RIFLE

This musket is something of an enigma. It was taken from a French drummer boy at the Battle of Waterloo in 1815. That in itself is odd as drummer boys were not equipped with muskets, needing both hands in action to beat their drums. For personal protection they had a short sword, which was often considered more useful for chopping firewood or butchering plundered livestock than it was as a weapon. But close inspection of the musket only deepens the mystery, as this is not the standard Napoleonic musket. Instead, it is a cut-down version of the Charleville Model, which entered service in 1717 and remained in production until 1777. What a drummer was doing with such a weapon in 1815 is a mystery.

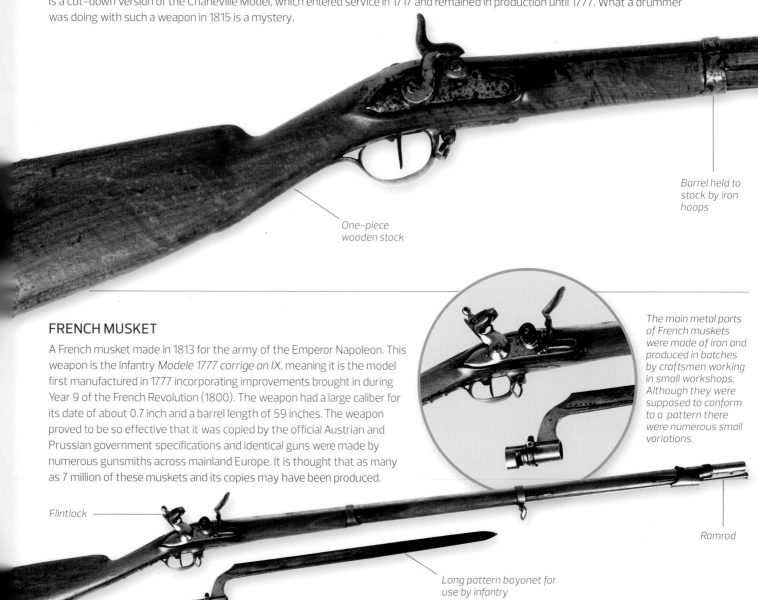

Barrel held to stock by iron hoops

One-piece wooden stock

FRENCH MUSKET

A French musket made in 1813 for the army of the Emperor Napoleon. This weapon is the Infantry *Modele 1777 corrige an IX*, meaning it is the model first manufactured in 1777 incorporating improvements brought in during Year 9 of the French Revolution (1800). The weapon had a large caliber for its date of about 0.7 inch and a barrel length of 59 inches. The weapon proved to be so effective that it was copied by the official Austrian and Prussian government specifications and identical guns were made by numerous gunsmiths across mainland Europe. It is thought that as many as 7 million of these muskets and its copies may have been produced.

The main metal parts of French muskets were made of iron and produced in batches by craftsmen working in small workshops. Although they were supposed to conform to a pattern there were numerous small variations.

Flintlock

Ramrod

Long pattern bayonet for use by infantry

THE BATTLE OF BUSSACO

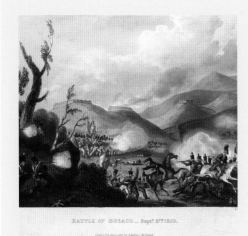

In 1810, the main road from Porto to Lisbon in Portugal climbed over a steep ridge known as the Serra do Bussaco. On September 27 a joint British–Portuguese army stood here under Wellington to block the advance of a much larger French army under Marshals Massena and Ney. The French attacked in two columns, which had the advantages of it being easier to maintain formation when marching over broken ground and allowing the advance to build up great momentum that was difficult to stop. It had won for French armies right across Europe. The waiting British formed up in line only three ranks deep. This formation was more difficult to keep in order, but had the advantage that every man could fire his musket at the enemy. The southern French column smashed through the British line, building momentum as it crested the ridge. At this critical moment Wellington brought up his reserves and overwhelmed the French with repeated volleys of musket fire.

Short barrel

Metal ramrod

Attachment for strap

ARAB MIQUELET

An Arab miquelet, probably from the late 18th century. The miquelet was a form of flintlock that had the mainspring on the outside of the lock and had a sear that locked the mechanism ready to be fired working horizontally, not vertically as on a true flintlock. The English name for this type of lock comes from the Spanish for militia and refers to the fact that in the Peninsular War several Spanish militia regiments had guns of this type. This example comes from North Africa. The barrel is held in place by silver wire and the butt stock is made of engraved ivory. The exposed mechanism, typical of the miquelet, is also heavily engraved and decorated.

Characteristic flared shoulder stock

Silvered bands hold barrel to stock

In a miquelet lock, the spring pushes down on the toe of the hammer, with sear knobs holding the hammer in position located at both the toe and the heel of the hammer.

Flat ivory shoulder plate

RIFLEMAN HARRIS

Shepherd Benjamin Harris joined the British Army in 1803, soon joining the new 95th Regiment. This new formation wore green uniforms, while most British units had redcoats, and was armed with the Baker Rifle. In 1808 he went to the Iberian Peninsula to join the British army fighting what was to become known as the Peninsular War. He fought at Rolica, Salamanca, Vimeiro, and Corunna before going to the Netherlands for the disastrous Walcheren Campaign. He left the army when peace came to Europe after the Battle of Waterloo and used his saved money to buy a cobbler's shop in the City of London. He later dictated his memoirs, being illiterate himself, and these were published in 1848 to become a much-read and highly valued account of the Napoleonic Wars seen from the ranks.

A Rifle Revolution

The Rifle Comes of Age

The 19th century has a reputation as a century of peace in Europe between the vast bloodshed of the Revolutionary Wars, which ended in 1815, and World War I, which began in 1914. In fact there were several smaller wars, but the general years of peace masked a rapid development of firearms technology. The percussion cap gave way to the integrated cartridge, which combined the percussion cap, main charge, and lead bullet into one packet encased in a thin jacket of copper. This development allowed breech–loading firearms to be developed, greatly increasing the rate of fire from three or four rounds a minute to ten or more.

GETTYSBURG: The Battle of Gettysburg proved to the turning point of the American Civil War. Although both sides lost about the same number of men, the Confederacy could not afford the losses and thereafter was forced to fight a defensive war with little prospect of eventual victory.

THE RIFLE COMES OF AGE

THE INDUSTRIAL REVOLUTION

The Industrial Revolution began in Britain in the mid-18th century, spreading slowly to other parts of the world with the USA, Germany, and France being among the first to take up the ideas of the revolution. The changes are often described in terms of technological innovations and working practices, but they were underpinned by a legal and financial framework, which ensured that those doing the hard work reaped the rewards, not those ensconced in influential political positions or born to privileged status. This "Anglo-Saxon" model of business and government was ridiculed by other societies, but they were keen to emulate the innovations to which it gave rise.

COLT LIGHTNING

Dating to 1884, the Colt Lightning was an attempt by the Colt company to break into the lucrative civilian repeating-rifle market, then dominated by Winchester. It was a good-quality weapon, though it was inclined to jam occasionally, but the unusual pump action proved to be unpopular and the weapon was discontinued in 1904. The rifle shown here had a barrel length of 26 inches and a 15-round magazine, while the carbine variant had a 20-inch barrel and a 12-round magazine. It was produced in a variety of calibers from .32 to .44.

Fore sight

Hammer

Elegantly shaped shoulder stock

The Lightning carbine held a 12- round magazine that was loaded by way of a spring-closed opening on the side of the plate in front of the trigger

HARPERS FERRY

In 1799, the US Government established an official Armory and Arsenal in the small Virginian town of Harpers Ferry. The area rapidly became an industrial center as hundreds of thousands of guns, swords, and other weapons were turned out for the US Army. This musket is undated, but was certainly produced before 1861, when the arms factory was destroyed during the US Civil War.

Percussion-cap mechanism

Fixings for strap

Trigger guard with integral shoulder-strap fiitting

The American Civil War

In 1860 Abraham Lincoln was elected to be President of the United States with a program to abolish slavery using federal legislation. Those living in states that relied on slave agricultural labor viewed this as a threat to their economic well-being and to states' rights. Eleven southern states seceded from the Union and joined together to form a Confederacy with looser ties between the states than the USA. Desperate to preserve the Union intact, Lincoln answered an armed challenge from

South Carolina by open warfare. The resulting war cost the lives of 600,000 American soldiers and ended with the utter defeat and economic ruin of the southern states. The majority of battlefield casualties were caused by small arms, with musketry begin the prime factor. The increasing accuracy of firearms, combined with the retention of centuries-old tactical deployments resulted in very high casualty rates for single actions. Toward the end of the war rapid fire guns such as the Gatling made the situation even worse.

GATLING GUN

Although often termed a machine gun, the Gatling Gun required a man to crank it and did not operate on the energy or gas created by the firing of bullets. It was, therefore, a rapid-fire weapon. As the handle was cranked, the six or ten barrels revolved around a central hub. As it moved, each barrel was in turn loaded and fired, and then ejected the spent cartridge. The cartridges fell into the barrels from a gravity-fed hopper mounted on top of the weapon. The gun was invented in 1861 by Richard Gatling and first saw service in the US Civil War. When true machine guns were invented in the 1890s, the Gatling went out of use.

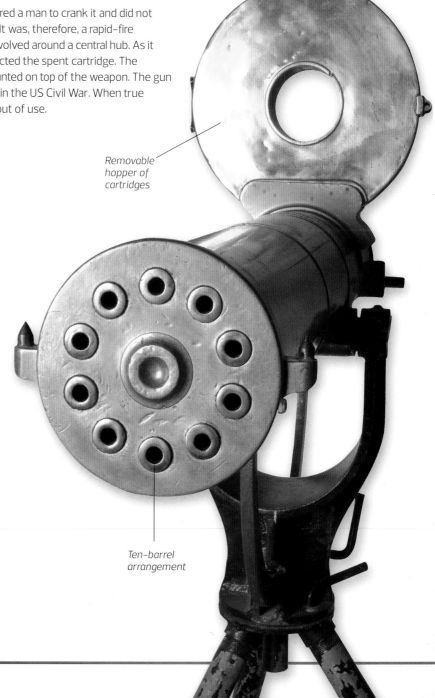

Removable hopper of cartridges

Ten-barrel arrangement

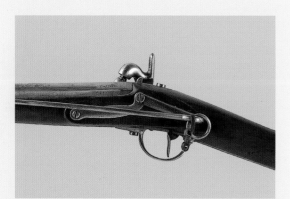

PERCUSSION-CAP FIRING SYSTEM

The percussion-cap system was developed in the 1820s and went out of use in the 1860s as metal cartridges were introduced. In essence, the percussion cap was simply another method of firing a muzzle-loaded barrel to replace the flintlock. Instead of having a flint striking powder to send a spark through the touch hole to the main charge, the percussion cap used a metal cap filled with fulminating chemicals that would explode when hit by a hammer. The extremely hot gasses thus created traveled down a tube to the main charge. This was a more reliable system than the flintlock, especially in damp weather.

BATTLE OF GETTYSBURG

Fought over three days in July 1863, the Battle of Gettysburg is generally considered to have been the turning point of the American Civil War. The failure of the Confederacy to mount a successful invasion of the North restricted them to a defensive strategy that enabled the Union to mobilize its greater resources. The climax of the battle came on the third day, when 12,500 Confederate infantry attacked the Unionist lines in what became known as Pickett's Charge, named after one of the generals who led the men forward. The infantry on both sides were armed mostly with percussion-cap rifles. The long range of these guns and open nature of the battlefield led to high casualties. The attacking Confederates suffered most, losing 50 percent of their men killed or wounded.

SPRINGFIELD

This musket dates to about 1830, but it has been greatly adapted and converted since it was first manufactured. It was made at the US Armory at Springfield, Massachusetts, as a traditional flintlock musket. When the US Army began converting to percussion weapons the older flintlock guns were put into storage or allocated to state militia. When the US Civil War broke out there was a sudden shortage of personal firearms. This was one of many muskets taken out of storage and hurriedly converted to have a percussion-cap firing system. At the same time the front third of the barrel was sawn off, perhaps to make what had been an infantry musket of more use to horsemen.

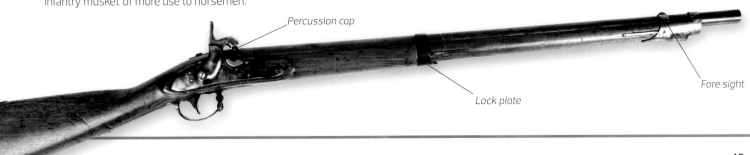

Percussion cap

Fore sight

Lock plate

Variations on a Theme

While the majority of early firearms adhered to a standard basic pattern and were made in or for heavily populated and technologically advanced areas such as Europe or China, some were produced to rather different designs for other markets. Given the technology of the time, these guns were not entirely divorced from those of the mainstream and, to the untrained eye, they might at first glance appear to be pretty much the same weapon. However, they were different enough to be considered quite separate types of weapon by contemporaries, who were more aware of the differences to the basic design than are immediately apparent to a person of the 21st century. These variations on the theme took many forms, some considerably better made than others.

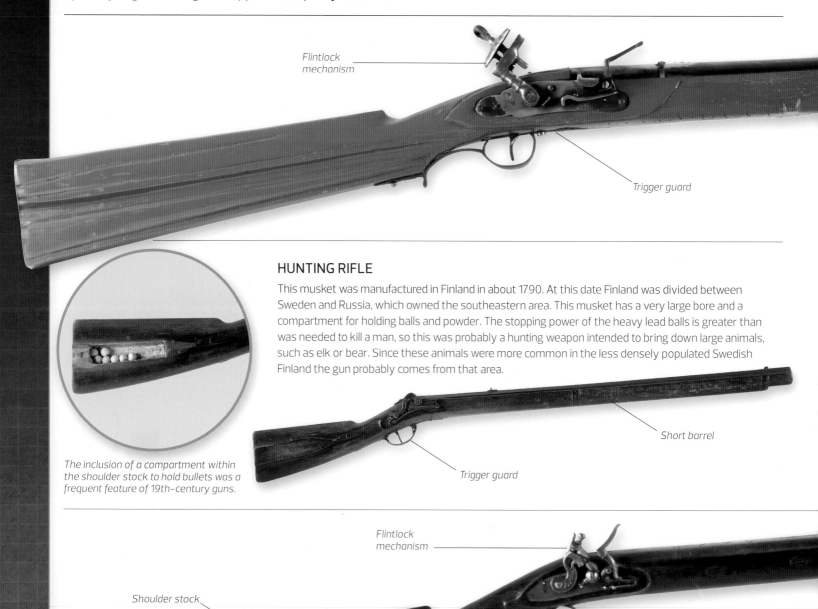

Flintlock mechanism

Trigger guard

The inclusion of a compartment within the shoulder stock to hold bullets was a frequent feature of 19th-century guns.

HUNTING RIFLE

This musket was manufactured in Finland in about 1790. At this date Finland was divided between Sweden and Russia, which owned the southeastern area. This musket has a very large bore and a compartment for holding balls and powder. The stopping power of the heavy lead balls is greater than was needed to kill a man, so this was probably a hunting weapon intended to bring down large animals, such as elk or bear. Since these animals were more common in the less densely populated Swedish Finland the gun probably comes from that area.

Short barrel

Trigger guard

Flintlock mechanism

Shoulder stock

AFRICAN TRADE RIFLE

The Venetian gunsmith Lazarino Cominazzo came from a dynasty of metalworkers that can be traced back to the early 1500s. During the 1660s he perfected a method of making elegantly-shaped barrels that could withstand the pressures created by a very heavy charge of powder. This enabled users to discharge balls at greater speeds, giving them a great range and stopping power. Adopting a distinctive shape for his barrels with an octagonal butt end and round muzzle, Cominazzo built up a huge and profitable business. By the time this gun was manufactured by his grandson, the Cominazzo were producing complete guns, of a standard much below that tolerated by the great Lazarino. This example was taken to Africa as a trade item.

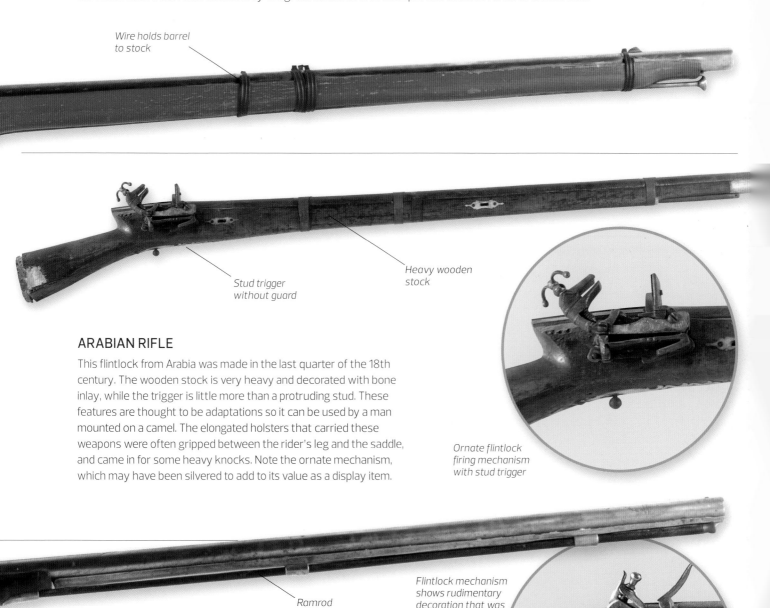

Wire holds barrel to stock

Stud trigger without guard

Heavy wooden stock

Ornate flintlock firing mechanism with stud trigger

ARABIAN RIFLE

This flintlock from Arabia was made in the last quarter of the 18th century. The wooden stock is very heavy and decorated with bone inlay, while the trigger is little more than a protruding stud. These features are thought to be adaptations so it can be used by a man mounted on a camel. The elongated holsters that carried these weapons were often gripped between the rider's leg and the saddle, and came in for some heavy knocks. Note the ornate mechanism, which may have been silvered to add to its value as a display item.

Ramrod

Flintlock mechanism shows rudimentary decoration that was popular in India.

INDIAN COMBINATION

Manufactured in India around 1825, this gun shows the difficulties experienced as the flintlock gave way to the percussion cap. Outwardly it is a fairly standard flintlock weapon, however a close inspection of the lock mechanism shows just how unusual this gun is. The lower portion of the cock that holds the flint has been shaped to be a hammer which strikes a nipple behind the flashpan where the percussion cap would sit. This dual system was adopted in areas, such as India, where the percussion caps could be in short supply.

Rifled Muskets

It has been known since ancient times that a missile will fly further and more accurately if it is made to spin in flight. Arrows and bolts were fitted with flight feathers to achieve this at least as early as 3000BC and probably much earlier. The earliest guns did not spin the missiles they shot but relied on the explosive power of the gunpowder and direction given by a barrel to get the ball to the right place. Experiments to spin a gun ball began early, perhaps around 1490, and by the 1560s some hunters were using muskets with barrels that had spiral grooves cut into the inside of the barrel to spin the ball they shot. This is called rifling. Practical difficulties in making the grooves accurately, and keeping them clean of the residue left by gunpowder, limited the use of the rifle. But while the rifle was slow to catch on, it ultimately won out over the musket.

GERMAN PERCUSSION-CAP RIFLE

This high quality German rifle was designed to take early metal cartridges fired by percussion cap. The latch under the barrel unclips to allow the barrel to swing sideways. A cartridge is then inserted, the barrel closed, and a percussion cap put over the nipple. After the gun has been fired, the barrel is opened again, the spent cartridge removed and the process repeated. The rifle came with a number of cartridges, each of which had to be filled and packed down by hand before loading.

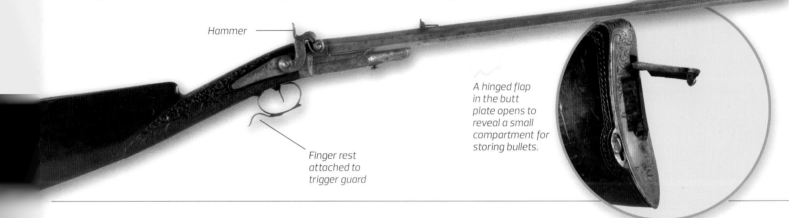

Hammer

A hinged flap in the butt plate opens to reveal a small compartment for storing bullets.

Finger rest attached to trigger guard

GERMAN HUNTING RIFLE

This hunting rifle made in Germany in the mid-19th century is unusual in that one barrel is rifled, while the other is a shotgun. Each barrel is operated by a separate trigger. Thus equipped, a hunter could tackle any opportunity that presented itself. If a boar or deer appeared he could use the rifle to send a bullet with accuracy to penetrate the hide and, hopefully, hit a vital organ. If a flight of birds went up, the shotgun would fire a cartridge of shot that would scatter to bring down the more delicate birds.

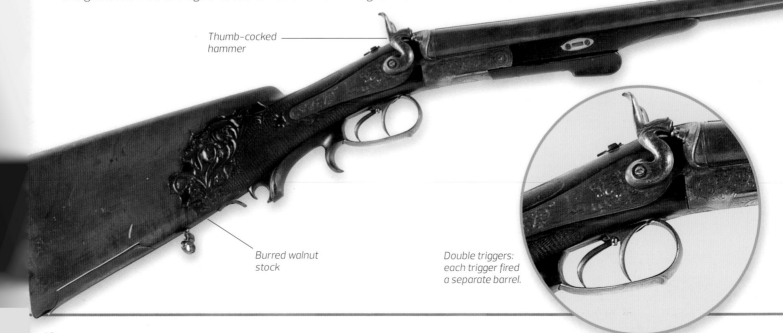

Thumb-cocked hammer

Burred walnut stock

Double triggers: each trigger fired a separate barrel.

BRUNSWICK RIFLE

The Brunswick rifle entered service with the British Army in 1838, only the second rifle to do so. Despite its name, the weapon has nothing to do with Brunswick in Germany but was produced at the Royal Small Arms Factory in Middlesex, in the south of England. The weapon had a bullet that featured two rounded lugs that fitted into large grooves within the barrel. This rather cumbersome arrangement was designed to overcome the problems with fouling that had affected earlier rifles. The rifle proved to be more accurate and more reliable than its rivals, though it was a heavier weapon. The stock of the Brunswick contained a compartment in which were stored ammunition and a small grease pot to lubricate the bullets and make them easier to load. The ramrod of the Brunswick was attached to the stock by a metal clip, which made it impossible to drop the rod accidentally in the broken country where riflemen were expected to operate. The muzzle also featured metal fixings to which a bayonet could be attached. The rifle saw several improvements introduced until production ceased in 1885.

The small indentation in the bullet compartment was to hold leather patches that were wrapped around each bullet to ensure that they fitted the rifling as tightly as possible.

The metal ramrod was necessary on the Brunswick because of the extra effort needed to push the snugly-fitting bullet down the barrel.

Heavy wooden stock

Trigger guard with loop for shoulder strap

BAKER RIFLE

Although widely known as the Baker Rifle after its inventor Ezekiel Baker, this weapon was officially the Pattern 1800 Infantry Rifle. It entered service with the British army in 1801 and remained the standard infantry rifle through to 1837. It fired a 0.615-inch lead ball and had a flintlock mechanism, which in later variants was replaced with a percussion-cap system.

Flintlock mechanism indicates that this is an early version

Metal ramrod with wide tip to help with loading

Trigger guard

European Rifles

Throughout the course of the 19th century, Europe enjoyed a longer period of general peace (1815–1914) than it had ever enjoyed previously. Nevertheless, there were a number of smaller scale conflicts within that time frame, such as the Crimean War and Franco-Prussian War, and it was these conflicts that drove forward a steady development in arms. The general trend was toward guns that were more reliable in battlefield conditions—especially damp weather—and which were accurate over longer and longer ranges.

DEATH RIDE OF MARS-LE-TOUR

On August 16, 1870, during the Franco-Prussian War, 30,000 Prussian and Hessian troops blundered into a massive French army of 130,000 men, thinking that they had only a retreating rearguard to deal with. As the German commander von Alvensieben sought to extricate his troops, he found he had committed all his infantry and artillery while large new French forces were advancing on his left flank. Facing disaster, he ordered his cavalry commander, von Bredow, to charge the advancing French. He led 800 horsemen from three regiments across 1,000 yards of open ground in the face of massed volleys from the French riflemen. Over 350 Germans were cut down by the rifle fire, but the survivors charged home with swords drawn, dispersed the French infantry, captured their artillery, and halted the advance. "The Death Ride" became a national legend in Germany.

BSA M1876

The Birmingham Small Arms (BSA) M1876 was a licensed copy of the Martini-Henry Pattern 1876 rifle. It was a single-shot, breech-loading rifle with a 20-inch barrel with a lever action so that when the lever was pulled down it opened the breech block. BSA was also a bicycle manufacturer and it sought to combine the two sides of its business by producing a version of the Roadster bicycle with fittings to carry the M1876. The idea was to give infantry additional mobility by mounting them on bicycles. The British War Office tried the idea, but discarded it. Half a century later, the Japanese would use bicycle troops to gain the edge of superior mobility over the British in Malaya, a factor largely responsible for their capture of Singapore in 1941.

The falling block mechanism had a scooped block which fell down when the lever was operated to open the rear of the barrel. The spent cartridge could then be removed and a new cartridge inserted.

Rear sight

Fore sight

Lever behind trigger to operate breech block

MARTINI-HENRY MKII

A Martini-Henry MkII manufactured in 1876. The lever action was a robust mechanism that allowed the user to fire 12 aimed shots a minute, even though this was a single-shot rifle. The rifle was designed for the British Army and first saw large-scale action in the Zulu War of 1879–80. It remained in service until 1888, after which the large number of rifles were used for training or passed on to the Indian Army and other forces in the British Empire. Although inaccurate at ranges over 500 yards, its robust construction and smooth operation meant that individual weapons remained in use. Today, Martini-Henrys are still to be found being wielded by Afghan fighters.

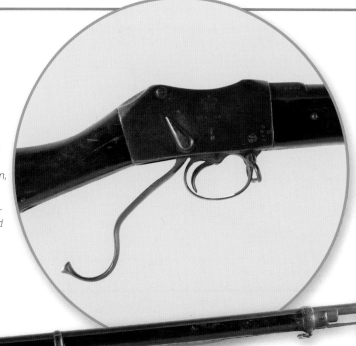

Loading lever in the open position. To load the rifle the user had to push the lever down, insert a cartridge into the rear of the barrel, and then pull the lever back up, which cocked the gun and made it ready to fire.

Iron bands secure barrel to stock

GEWEHR

An example of the Gewehr 1888 German rifle with the bolt action open. This rifle was developed to make use of the new smokeless powder. Not only was this propellant more powerful than the old gunpowder, it produced virtually no fouling soot to clog the barrel. The greater power allowed the rifle to have a smaller caliber of 7.92mm, while retaining the stopping power of the older larger bores by means of a greater muzzle velocity. The rifle first saw service when German troops intervened in China's Boxer Rebellion of 1899 and was still the primary German infantry rifle at the outbreak of World War I.

This rifle was loaded by pulling the bolt fully back to open up a slot in the top of the rifle. A clip of 5 rounds could then be pushed down into this slot to fill the magazine. As each round was fired the clip rose up and eventually was ejected when empty.

Rear sight

Fore sight

Integral box magazine

Strap swivel

VETTERLI

A Swiss Vetterli Model 1878 rifle. This is a minor upgrade of the Model 1869 and was recognized to be the most advanced military rifle of its day. The rifle featured a tubular magazine and a self-cocking mechanism that increased the rate of fire to 21 aimed rounds per minute. The 1878 model had an internal hammer, one of the first put into production, and more rounded metal fittings. The Italian army adopted a version of the Vetterli, which was abandoned in 1907, then brought out of storage in 1915 as Italy faced a desperate shortage of rifles when it entered World War I on the side of the Allies.

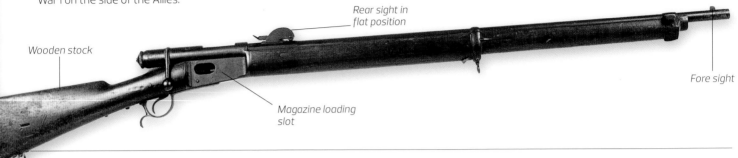

Rear sight in flat position

Wooden stock

Fore sight

Magazine loading slot

KRAG

A Krag-Jorgensen bolt-action repeating rifle of 1889. This Norwegian weapon had a particularly smooth action and was adopted as the standard infantry rifle by the armies of Norway, Denmark, and the USA. A unique feature was the side-mounted magazine with a metal cover on the right side of the breech. Unlike other guns of the time, the user did not need to place cartridges carefully in to the magazine. Instead, he needed only to open the cover, push the cartridges in, and close the cover again. The internal layout and mechanism then ensured the cartridges were fed into the firing chamber.

Magazine holds 5 rounds

Barrel length 32¾ inches

Webbed strap

SNIDER ENFIELD

The Snider-Enfield was the first breech-loading rifle to enter service with the British Army, in 1867. It took its name from the fact that it combined the breech-loading mechanism invented by American Jacob Snider with the rifle produced by the armaments factory at Enfield. Breech loading required a new type of ammunition. At the rear end of the barrel was a metal block that the user removed to enable him to pull out the spent cartridge and insert a new one. The block was then replaced and the hammer pulled back, ready for firing.

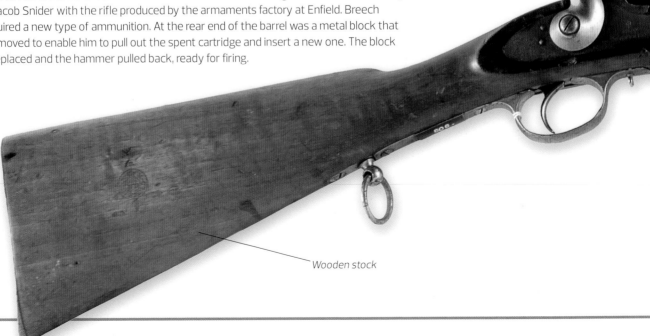

Wooden stock

BATTLE OF ISANDHLWANA

On January 22, 1879, 20,000 Zulus armed mostly with spears attacked 1,800 British and colonial troops armed with the Martini–Henry rifle. The initial Zulu advance was halted by sustained volleys of rifle fire, but the defensive fire then slackened and the Zulus charged to overwhelm and annihilate the British. There were few British survivors, but an inquiry suggested that the boxes holding the Martini–Henry ammunition were so tightly screwed down to render them watertight that they could not be opened fast enough. Later experience showed that after several shots had been fired, the Martini–Henry was prone to jam as the breech block heated up, so this may have been the cause of the defeat.

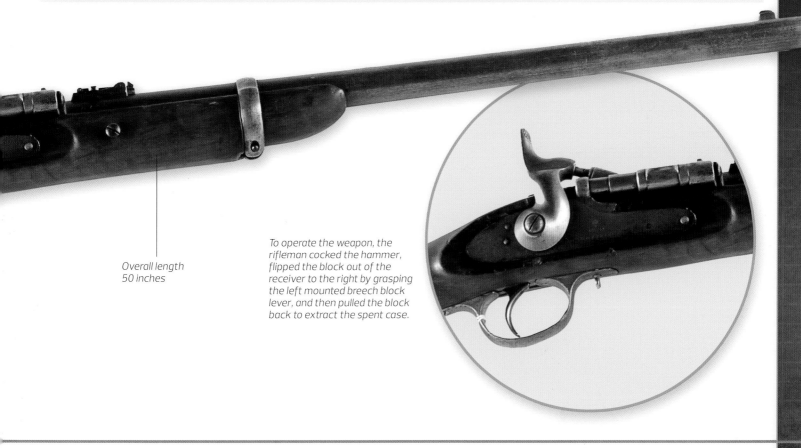

*Overall length
50 inches*

To operate the weapon, the rifleman cocked the hammer, flipped the block out of the receiver to the right by grasping the left mounted breech block lever, and then pulled the block back to extract the spent case.

American Repeating Rifles

During the second half of the 19th century the American civilian market was booming for gun makers such as Winchester, Colt, and Remington. In many areas of the USA law enforcement was haphazard, so banks, railroads, and other business felt the need to provide their own armed protection. Farmers and ranchers faced more natural hazards to themselves and their livestock in the shape of bears, pumas, and wolves, while the vast wilderness areas provided plentiful opportunities for hunting. Spending their own money, these gun users wanted to acquire good quality guns at reasonable prices. This in turn drove the manufacturers not only to produce the desired weapons, but also to gain publicity for their products.

TROWEL BAYONET

An American military rifle fitted with the unusual trowel bayonet invented by Colonel Edmund Rice. This weapon was designed to be a multi–purpose piece of equipment in the infantryman's arsenal. Its two primary purposes were to be used as an offensive weapon and to dig entrenchments, though men also found it useful to cut firewood, produce tent pegs, and plaster walls. Over 10,000 of these were issued by the US Army from 1870 onward, but it eventually proved to be adequate at several tasks, but good at none of them. In 1881 it was withdrawn.

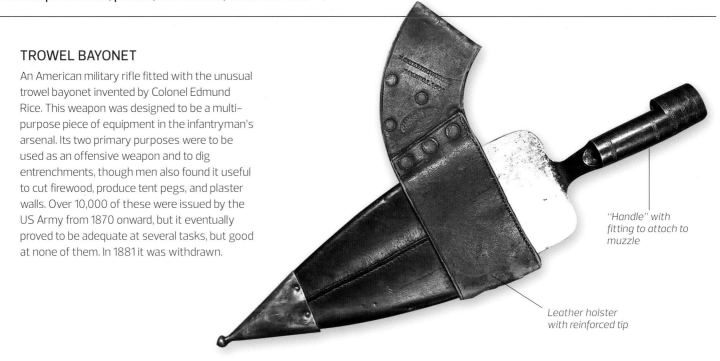

"Handle" with fitting to attach to muzzle

Leather holster with reinforced tip

ARGENTINE MAUSER

The 91 Argentine, a rifle produced by the Mauser company. The design was originally intended for the 1884 Bavarian Arms Trials in the hope that it would be chosen to equip the Bavarian Army. The Mauser failed to win that contract, but there were many international observers at the trials and this model of Mauser attracted the attention of the Argentinian military, then looking for a replacement for its aging Remington rifles. The rifle used the new concept of a rimless cartridge to ensure smooth feeding from a box cartridge.

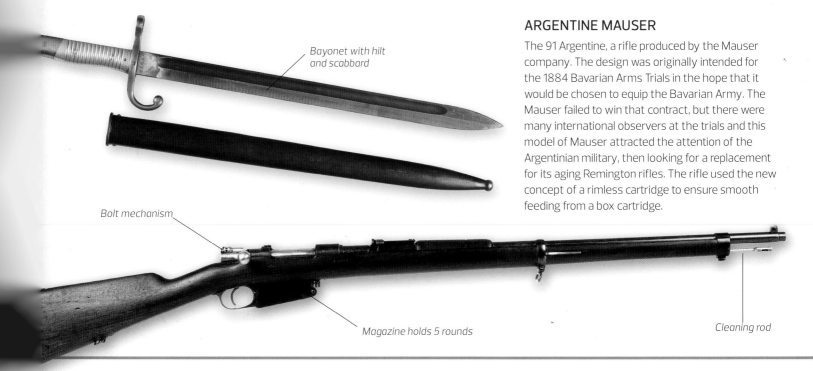

Bayonet with hilt and scabbard

Bolt mechanism

Magazine holds 5 rounds

Cleaning rod

PARKER RIFLE

This short rifle is typical of the sort of weapons carried by some regiments during the Civil War. The sudden demand for large quantities of weaponry meant that the states had to buy what they could get, including this Parker-Hale rifle from Birmingham, England. This is a muzzle-loading gun that fires a .451 slug. The rifling twists at a ratio of 1:20, giving the slug a modest spin as it was fired. As with many rifles of this date, the fouling of the rifling grooves was a constant problem, so cleaning the weapon was one of the soldiers most frequent tasks.

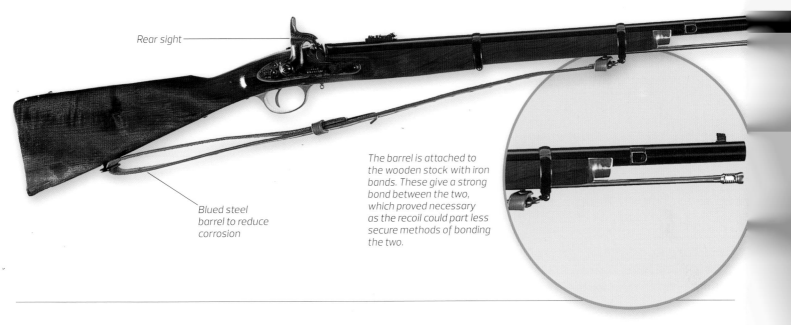

Rear sight

Blued steel barrel to reduce corrosion

The barrel is attached to the wooden stock with iron bands. These give a strong bond between the two, which proved necessary as the recoil could part less secure methods of bonding the two.

WHITNEY RIFLE

Made by the Whitney Arms Company, founded by the inventor Eli Whitney who is better known for his contributions to the textile industry, this carbine was manufactured in 1864 for the use of the US Navy. The barrel is comparatively heavy for a carbine, an effort to stop the barrel from heating up after repeated firing. It is a muzzle-loading weapon and although like all such weapons was relatively inaccurate, it has both a fore sight and rear sight to facilitate more precise aiming.

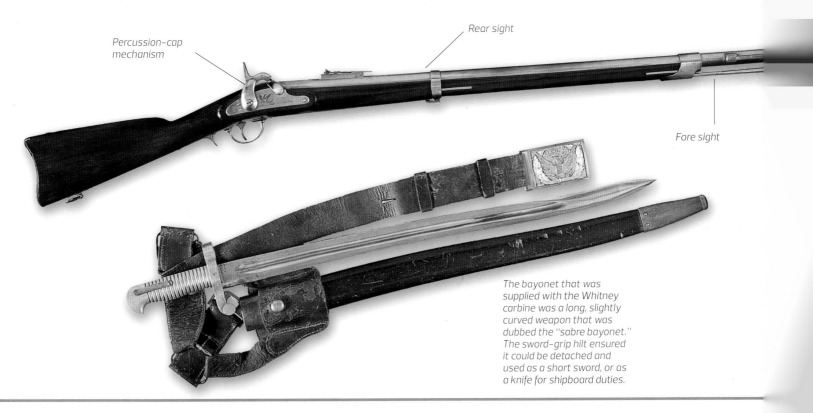

Rear sight

Percussion-cap mechanism

Fore sight

The bayonet that was supplied with the Whitney carbine was a long, slightly curved weapon that was dubbed the "sabre bayonet." The sword-grip hilt ensured it could be detached and used as a short sword, or as a knife for shipboard duties.

REMINGTON RIFLE

A Model 24 Remington rifle that uses the Browning movement. This a .22 gun designed for the sporting market. It has a takedown design, meaning that the barrel can be removed without the need for special tools, making it easy to be partially dismantled for transport to and from firing ranges.

Dismantling attachments

Trigger guard

WINCHESTER PRESENTATION RIFLE

A unique presentation version of the Winchester M1866 made by the company for Maximilian, Emperor of Mexico. The rifle has an ivory stock, gold-plated lock cover, and is engraved with the Mexican eagle. Such presentation pieces were a vital piece of publicity and marketing for the company, allowing them to boast that famous men used their weapons on particular occasions. This particular gun did its imperial recipient little good. He was captured by rebels and, on June 19, 1867, was shot by firing squad.

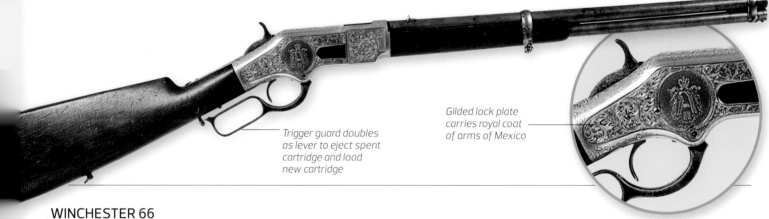

Trigger guard doubles as lever to eject spent cartridge and load new cartridge

Gilded lock plate carries royal coat of arms of Mexico

WINCHESTER 66

The Winchester Model 1866 was a ground-breaking rifle due to its 15-shot magazine and lever action, which allowed the user to fire a number of shots without needing to stop to reload. It was dubbed "The Yellowboy," as its receiver was made of a yellow bronze alloy. This example is a presentation piece sent to Czar Alexander II of Russia and engraved with Russian Imperial symbols. This is rather ironic, as the Russians were defeated at the Siege of Plevna in 1877 by Turkish defenders armed with these repeating rifles, while the Russians had only single-shot Czech Krnka rifles. The action at Plevna caused most nations to adopt a repeating rifle for their infantry, although only Turkey and Switzerland bought such weapons from the Winchester company.

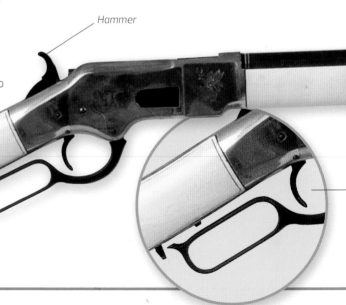

Hammer

BATTLE OF SAN JUAN HILL

Fought on July 1, 1898, the Battle of San Juan Hill was the bloodiest battle of the Spanish-American War. The Spanish infantry were equipped with Mauser M1893 rifles, the Americans with the Krag–Jorgensen. At first the Spanish rifle fire from entrenchments on the hill crest halted the American advance, inflicting heavy casualties. However, Colonel (later US President) Theodore Roosevelt noticed a weakness in the layout of the Spanish trenches. Supported by Gatling guns, Roosevelt led his men in a charge that secured a toehold on the hill. Seeing this, the rest of the American army advanced and drove the Spanish in retreat. Despite their victory, the Americans recognized the weakness of their rifles and soon discarded the Krag and adopted the Mauser.

Shoulder– strap fitting

The lever action of the Winchester 66 allowed cartridges to be ejected and reloaded without time-consuming fiddling about by the user and earned this gun the name of "repeater."

Cartridges were loaded into the tube magazine by way of this opening, the magazine itself being housed within the forestock.

Winchester 73

The most famous weapon the Winchester company ever made was the Model 1873, widely known simply as "The 73." It was at first available only for the .44–40 cartridge, but demand from the public soon caused Winchester to introduce versions for the .38–40 and .32–20 cartridges that were used in many types of popular handgun. This meant that men riding far from sources of new cartridges needed to carry only one type of ammunition for both their rifle and their handgun. Winchester's marketing plan included making prestigious presentation weapons for such notables as Czar Alexander II of Russia and King Edward VII of Great Britain.

ROYAL WINCHESTER
A presentation weapon from the Winchester company. This example is a Winchester 1873 sent to the Prince of Wales, later King Edward VII. It has a special blued finish to its metal parts plus a silver medallion set into the butt. Edward was a keen hunter, shooting big game in India and elsewhere in the British Empire as well as shooting vast numbers of game birds at his country estate of Sandringham, Norfolk. It is not clear, however, if he ever used this particular weapon.

OLIVER WINCHESTER

Born in Boston in 1810, Oliver Fisher Winchester originally made his fortune as a clothing manufacture. As his clothing business flourished he invested in the Volcanic Repeating Arms Company and took control of that firm in 1856, later renaming it the Winchester Repeating Arms Co. Following the Civil War Oliver Winchester introduced the Model 1866 and then had his greatest success with the introduction of the hugely popular Winchester 73, one of the most celebrated guns of the West. Oliver Winchester died in 1881.

A view of the Winchester 73 lever action with the side plates removed.

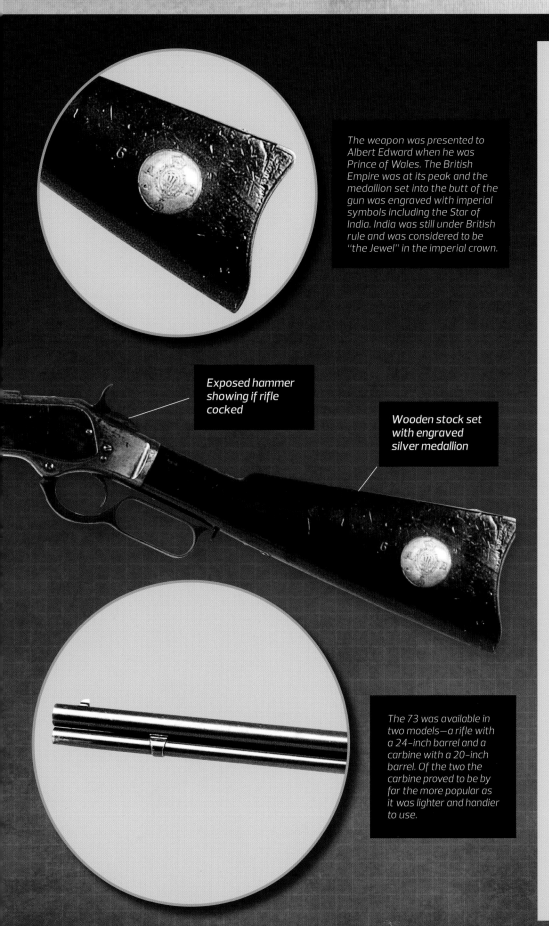

The weapon was presented to Albert Edward when he was Prince of Wales. The British Empire was at its peak and the medallion set into the butt of the gun was engraved with imperial symbols including the Star of India. India was still under British rule and was considered to be "the Jewel" in the imperial crown.

Exposed hammer showing if rifle cocked

Wooden stock set with engraved silver medallion

The 73 was available in two models—a rifle with a 24-inch barrel and a carbine with a 20-inch barrel. Of the two the carbine proved to be by far the more popular as it was lighter and handier to use.

WINCHESTER '73, THE MOVIE

As well as producing magnificent presentation weapons for the rich and powerful, the Winchester Rifle company used many other inventive marketing strategies to promote their rifles. The company test-fired all barrels and those with the tightest grouping of shots were fitted to premier mechanisms and marketed as "One in One Thousand" guns to be sold at a premium price. Only 136 such weapons were produced of the highly regarded Model 1876.

In 1950, Winchester's most successful rifle enjoyed a new kind of celebrity with the production of the Hollywood western "Winchester '73." The movie starred James Stewart and Shelley Winters and followed the story of one such gun through the hands of its various owners. These included cowboys, Native Americans, lawmen, and bandits.

The publicity drive for the movie included a campaign to find surviving copies of the One in One Thousand Winchester 73 rifles. Only a handful were found and these were put on display at major cinemas.

Carbines

Weapons for Horsemen

Many mounted men carried a short musket, or a musket that had had its end cut off, but it seems to have been the French who first developed regiments of horsemen specifically to use the carbine. These units, known as *carabiniers-à-cheval*, were first recruited in about 1570. They were equipped as light cavalry, but with the addition of carbines. Their role was to scout ahead of the army, like light cavalry, but to be able to engage in fire fights with enemy troops as well. Their firepower came as a nasty shock to enemy armies, who quickly copied the idea. The carabiniers-à-cheval remained elite units within the French army until they were amalgamated with heavy cavalry regiments in 1871.

THE BATTLE of the Little Big Horn in 1876 pitched the US 7th Cavalry armed with Springfield 1873 carbines against a much greater number of Cheyenne and Lakota armed with a wide variety of weapons from stone axes to modern Winchester repeating rifles. The performance of the Springfield carbine has often been cited as a reason for the defeat of the 7th Cavalry.

Early Carbines

Cavalry traditionally fought with cold steel or with pistols. The complex caracole tactic saw light cavalry armed with pistols advance at a trot, fire their weapons at the enemy and then turn aside to make space for the next rank to fire. When the enemy formation was sufficiently disrupted, heavy cavalry would charge home with lance or sword to complete the onslaught.

By the 17th century the caracole had been abandoned. Instead all horsemen were equipped similarly, though they were still divided into light and heavy cavalry. Each man had a sword (rarely a lance) plus a musket and sometimes a pistol or two. The cavalry were expected to scout ahead of the army, and to skirmish in battle, using the musket, as well as to fight in pitched battles using their swords. Before long it was found that a musket was too long and unwieldy to use on horseback or to pull quickly from a saddle holster. The answer was the shorter carbine.

Catch to hold bayonet in place when not in use.

Spring-loaded bayonet

Tough wooden stock made from walnut timber

BLUNDERBUSS WITH SPRING-LOADED BAYONET

This short weapon is typical of an early effort to solve the problem of giving a horseman firepower more effective than a pistol, though this particular example is quite late dating to 1806. It is effectively a short blunderbuss fitted with a bayonet. Firing a concentrated packet of small shot— rather like a sawn off shotgun—this weapon would have been horribly effective at short range, but almost useless at ranges over 15 yards. Like the bayonet itself, therefore, this weapon was primarily for close-quarters combat.

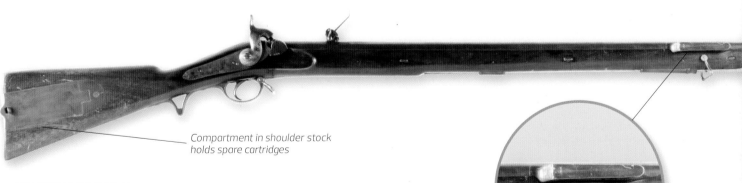

Compartment in shoulder stock holds spare cartridges

BRUNSWICK RIFLE

The Brunswick rifle was, despite its name, a British weapon that was developed in the 1830s and entered mass production in the 1840s. In the British Army it was primarily an infantry weapon, but in other countries it was often considered as a cavalry weapon. The heavy weight of the gun—over 10 pounds—meant that a horse was better able to carry the weight than a man. The barrel was relatively short, being 30 inches when most infantry guns were over 40 inches, which also made it more convenient for use by horsemen. This particular example was manufactured in Britain in 1843, but was used in the Russian Army.

Ramrod secured to barrel by clip to prevent it being lost in action

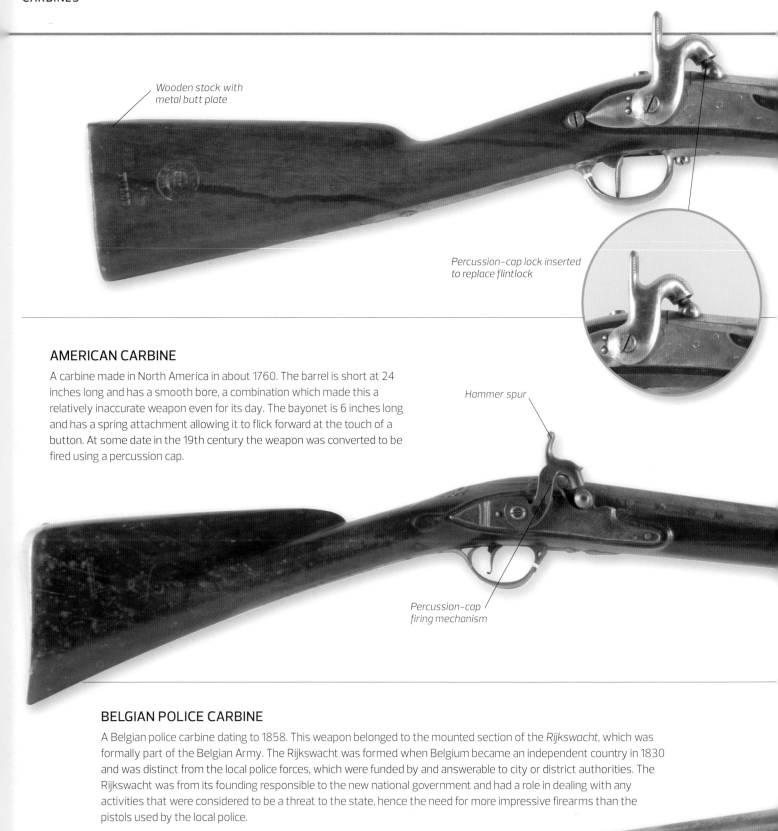

Wooden stock with metal butt plate

Percussion-cap lock inserted to replace flintlock

AMERICAN CARBINE

A carbine made in North America in about 1760. The barrel is short at 24 inches long and has a smooth bore, a combination which made this a relatively inaccurate weapon even for its day. The bayonet is 6 inches long and has a spring attachment allowing it to flick forward at the touch of a button. At some date in the 19th century the weapon was converted to be fired using a percussion cap.

Hammer spur

Percussion-cap firing mechanism

BELGIAN POLICE CARBINE

A Belgian police carbine dating to 1858. This weapon belonged to the mounted section of the *Rijkswacht*, which was formally part of the Belgian Army. The Rijkswacht was formed when Belgium became an independent country in 1830 and was distinct from the local police forces, which were funded by and answerable to city or district authorities. The Rijkswacht was from its founding responsible to the new national government and had a role in dealing with any activities that were considered to be a threat to the state, hence the need for more impressive firearms than the pistols used by the local police.

Short barrel

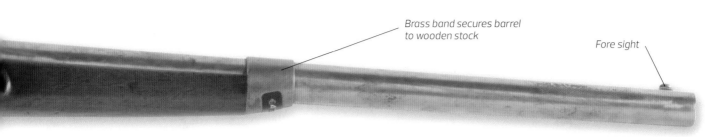

Brass band secures barrel to wooden stock

Fore sight

MUTZIG FRENCH CAVALRY CARBINE

This cavalry carbine was manufactured as a flintlock weapon in 1822. In 1835 it was converted to the percussion-cap system. It features a large metal ring (not visible) that allows it to be attached to the saddle by a leather strap for swift use. The gun comes from the *Manufacture Imperiale d'Armes de Mutzig*, an official French military arsenal which was built in the grounds of an old medieval castle that had lost its defensive potential in the face of heavy artillery. After the Franco-Prussian War of 1870 Mutzig, along with the rest of Alsace, was annexed by Germany. The armory passed to the Kaiser, who built a massive fortress near the town.

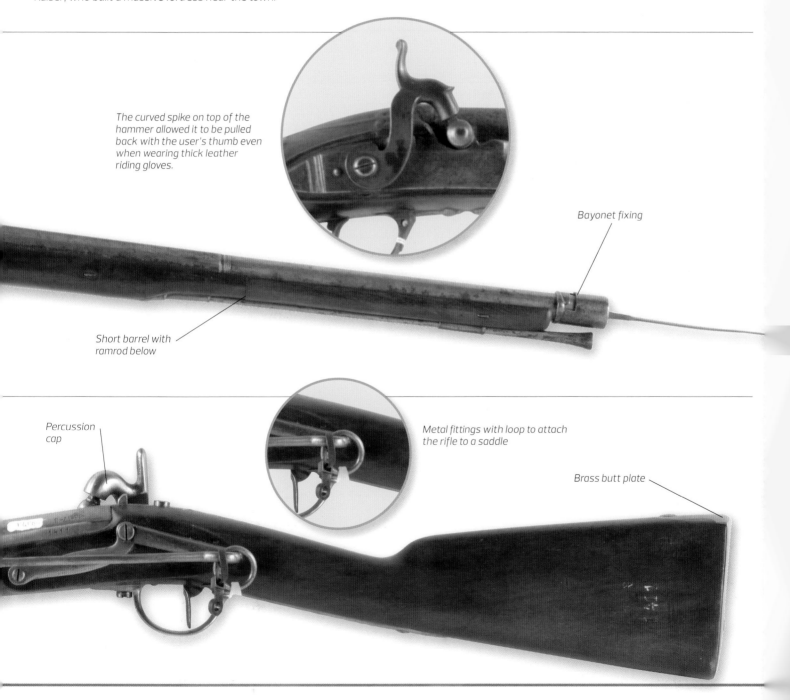

The curved spike on top of the hammer allowed it to be pulled back with the user's thumb even when wearing thick leather riding gloves.

Bayonet fixing

Short barrel with ramrod below

Percussion cap

Metal fittings with loop to attach the rifle to a saddle

Brass butt plate

BRITISH 1796 PATTERN CARBINE

The shorter musket issued to cavalry regiments was generally very similar to those issued to infantry units in the same army. However, there were some differences in addition to the shorter barrel length. There was often a large metal ring attached to the stock near the lock mechanism. This held a leather strap that was attached to the saddle so that if the weapon were to be dropped in action it would not be entirely lost.

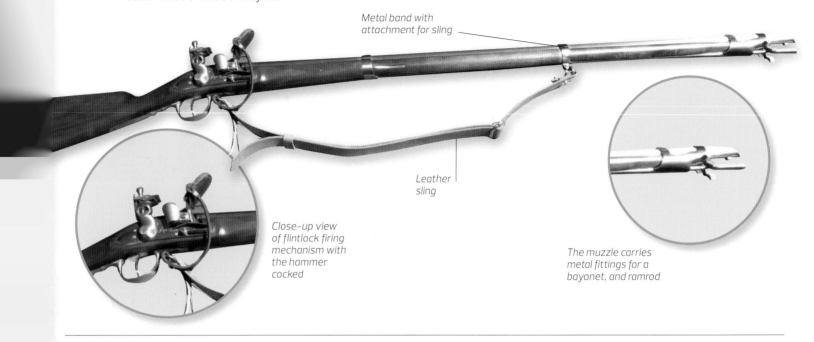

Metal band with attachment for sling

Leather sling

Close-up view of flintlock firing mechanism with the hammer cocked

The muzzle carries metal fittings for a bayonet, and ramrod

SEA SERVICE CARBINE

The Royal Navy had rifles about six inches shorter than the British Army because of the low ceilings and cramped conditions on board ship. From 1778 to 1860 the Sea Service carbine was identical to the Land Pattern "Brown Bess" musket in all details other than its length. While most of these sea carbines were issued to Marines, a number of sailors in each ship would be fully trained in their use and would be equipped with them when fighting ashore or during close action against other ships.

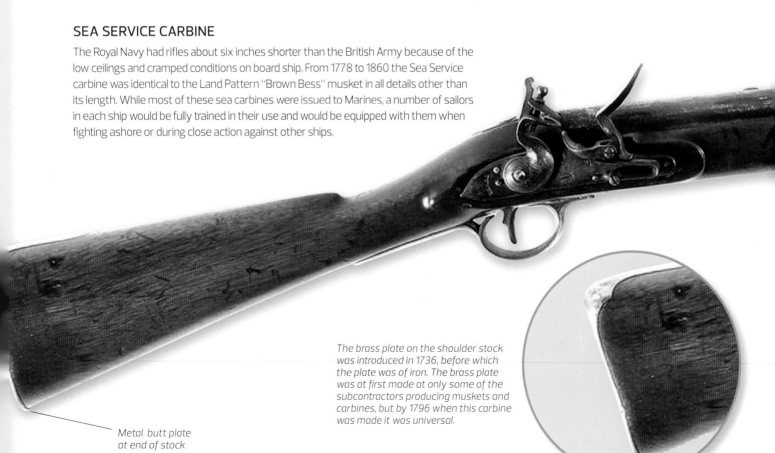

The brass plate on the shoulder stock was introduced in 1736, before which the plate was of iron. The brass plate was at first made at only some of the subcontractors producing muskets and carbines, but by 1796 when this carbine was made it was universal.

Metal butt plate at end of stock

MARSHAL NEY

Although he is today best remembered as one of Napoleon's marshals, Marshal Michel Ney began his military career in 1787 as a hussar. As such he was armed with sabre and carbine and mounted on a small, fast horse. Ney rose rapidly through the ranks to become an officer, reaching general rank in 1796. He believed in leading from the front, which earned him the nickname of "Bravest of the Brave," but his courage also led to several injuries and to being thrown from his horse and being captured.

Throughout his career, Ney showed a keen appreciation of what cavalry could do with carbines, especially when fighting rearguard actions. His handling of the rearguard at the River Beresina as the French sought to retreat from Russia in 1812 was particularly highly regarded. He was himself the last man to cross the bridge and leave Russia. Many tacticians believe his best rearguard action was fought at Casal Novo in Portugal in 1811. Ney put his infantry and artillery on a ridge to delay the British advance long enough for the main French army to get over the River Ceira, but first hid the 3rd Hussars forward of his position where they would be invisible to the British. The advancing British infantry were still in column of march when Ney unleashed his hussars, who inflicted heavy casualties before the arrival of the British cavalry forced their retreat. Ney then held the British assault on his ridge until dusk, after which his men slipped away over the river.

Iron ramrod

37-inch barrel

The iron moving pieces of the lock mechanism were prone to rusting at sea where the salt water could get into the workings. It was customary for the guns to be supplied well greased and for cleaning to be regular and thorough.

Cavalry Carbines

The distinguishing feature of the cavalry carbine was the overall length of the weapon. When slung in its long holster on the saddle, the gun had to be positioned with the butt upward and close to the rider's hand so that it could be quickly pulled out for use. At the same time the butt had to be positioned below the elbow so that it did not interfere in the hand movements needed to control the horse. Similarly the muzzle had to be high enough so that it did not get in the way of the horse's legs and hooves, even in a high-stepping trot. The name is thought to derive from two regiments of French cavalry in the 1690s who were armed with short muskets by their commander the Duc de Maine. The regiments proved to be so effective that they were nicknamed *Les Carrabins*, or "The Gravediggers," and the name was by the 1730s transferred from the regiments to the weapon.

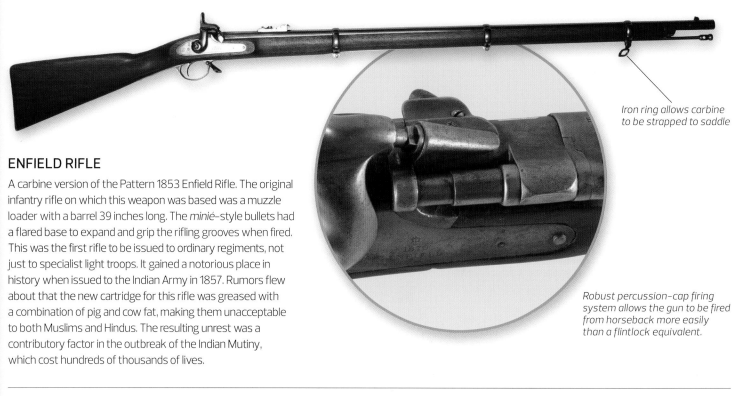

Iron ring allows carbine to be strapped to saddle

Robust percussion-cap firing system allows the gun to be fired from horseback more easily than a flintlock equivalent.

ENFIELD RIFLE

A carbine version of the Pattern 1853 Enfield Rifle. The original infantry rifle on which this weapon was based was a muzzle loader with a barrel 39 inches long. The *minié*-style bullets had a flared base to expand and grip the rifling grooves when fired. This was the first rifle to be issued to ordinary regiments, not just to specialist light troops. It gained a notorious place in history when issued to the Indian Army in 1857. Rumors flew about that the new cartridge for this rifle was greased with a combination of pig and cow fat, making them unacceptable to both Muslims and Hindus. The resulting unrest was a contributory factor in the outbreak of the Indian Mutiny, which cost hundreds of thousands of lives.

Rifle bolt pulled back to open the breech for cleaning or reloading

Rear sight

Fore sight

Bayonet fixing assembly

TORINO 1882 RIFLE WITH BAYONET

A Model 1871 Vetterli cavalry carbine. It is marked "Torino 1882" indicating that it was made in the company's Turin factory in that year. The Model 1871 was an improvement on the original Model 1867, which featured a center-fire cartridge as opposed to a rim-fire cartridge and changes to the magazine. Although manufactured in Italy, the company designations for its models were in German as the company was based in German-speaking parts of Switzerland. This carbine for the Italian cavalry was therefore the *Kavallerie-Repetierkarabiner*. The long bayonet is from the light infantry *stutzer* variant, which was not issued to the cavalry.

Revolving cylinder based on Colt pistol original

Barrel cut down from original length of 24 inches

Forward hand grip

COLT MODEL 1855 CARBINE

This model was based on the popular and effective sidehammer–pistol revolver mechanism, but with a longer barrel and shoulder stock. The model was produced in both the short-barreled carbine and the long-barreled rifle. The carbine used paper cartridges, each pushed individually into the chambers of the revolving drum. Percussion caps were then put over the rear of each chamber. Although the gun worked well in trials, on campaign with the army it was soon found to have a serious flaw. Frequent reloading with paper cartridges could cause some loose powder to get caught in the revolving mechanism. This meant that when the trigger was pulled the spark from the percussion cap not only fired the chamber under the hammer, but also the trapped powder, which in turn could set off one or more of the other chambers. Soldiers naturally objected to spare bullets flying about and the weapon was removed from use.

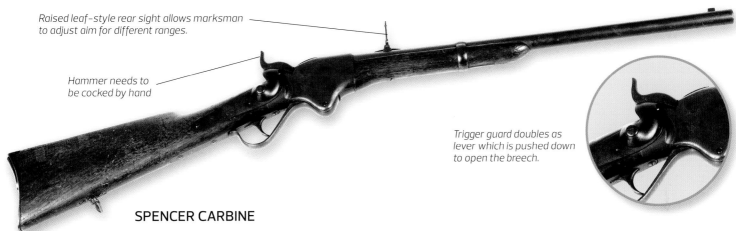

Raised leaf-style rear sight allows marksman to adjust aim for different ranges.

Hammer needs to be cocked by hand

Trigger guard doubles as lever which is pushed down to open the breech.

SPENCER CARBINE

A Spencer Model 1860 carbine. This was a shortened version of the Spencer repeating rifle and was intended for use by the US Cavalry. The tubular magazine of this carbine held seven cartridges and could be rapidly refilled from a special cartridge box designed to allow the cartridges to flow smoothly into the magazine. Despite these features the US War Department declined to place orders until President Abraham Lincoln tried the weapon for himself. Once in action the carbine proved to be reliable, although the large amount of smoke it created sometimes hampered its effective use by cavalry.

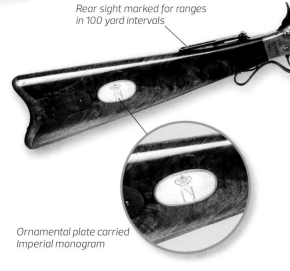

Rear sight marked for ranges in 100 yard intervals

Ornamental plate carried Imperial monogram

MASSACHUSETTS ARMS

A presentation example of the 1851 Maynard carbine made for French Emperor Napoleon III, whose badge of a crowned "N" appears on a silver plate on the butt. This example was hand finished to work smoothly and all components were specially checked to ensure top quality for the prestigious recipient, but otherwise it is a standard model. The carbine, and the rifle on which it was based had a revolutionary loading system for its time. When the loading lever was pushed it raised the barrel for the old cartridge case to be removed and a new cartridge inserted. When the lever was raised the barrel closed and a percussion cap was pushed forward on to the nipple to make the gun ready for firing. Huge numbers were bought by the state militias in the 1850s, so the gun saw widespread use in the US Civil War.

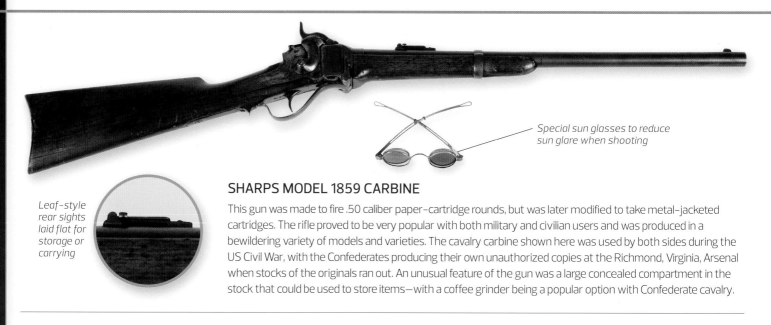

Special sun glasses to reduce sun glare when shooting

Leaf-style rear sights laid flat for storage or carrying

SHARPS MODEL 1859 CARBINE

This gun was made to fire .50 caliber paper-cartridge rounds, but was later modified to take metal-jacketed cartridges. The rifle proved to be very popular with both military and civilian users and was produced in a bewildering variety of models and varieties. The cavalry carbine shown here was used by both sides during the US Civil War, with the Confederates producing their own unauthorized copies at the Richmond, Virginia, Arsenal when stocks of the originals ran out. An unusual feature of the gun was a large concealed compartment in the stock that could be used to store items—with a coffee grinder being a popular option with Confederate cavalry.

BELGIAN CARBINE

A carbine produced for the Belgian cavalry in the 1860s. This is a relatively unsophisticated, single-shot weapon. When Belgium became independent in 1830 the new kingdom declared itself to be perpetually neutral and, to avoid causing offence to any of its much larger neighbors, did not form an army at all. After a wave of revolutions swept Europe in 1848, King Leopold I decided that Belgium did need an army after all and a small armed force was raised. This basic weapon was typical of the poor-quality equipment issued to that army. After the Franco-Prussian War of 1870 the Belgian army was hastily enlarged and thoroughly modernized, with weapons such as this being discarded.

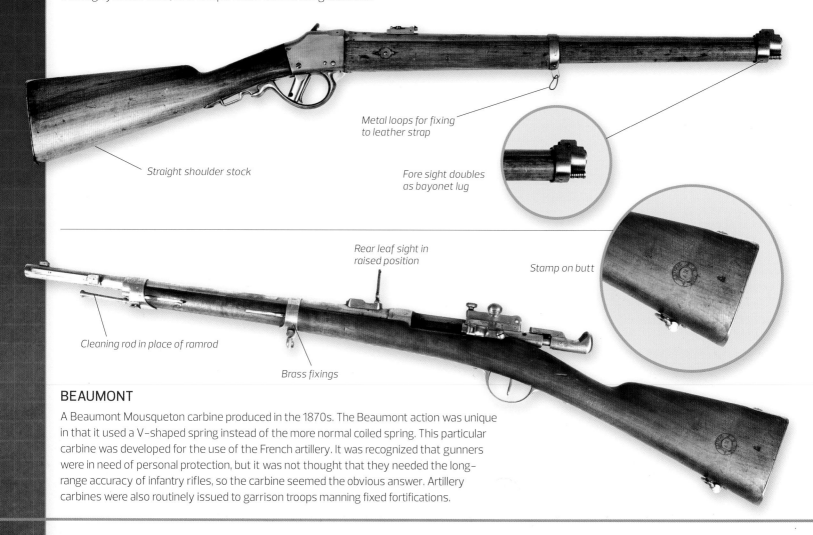

Metal loops for fixing to leather strap

Straight shoulder stock

Fore sight doubles as bayonet lug

Rear leaf sight in raised position

Stamp on butt

Cleaning rod in place of ramrod

Brass fixings

BEAUMONT

A Beaumont Mousqueton carbine produced in the 1870s. The Beaumont action was unique in that it used a V-shaped spring instead of the more normal coiled spring. This particular carbine was developed for the use of the French artillery. It was recognized that gunners were in need of personal protection, but it was not thought that they needed the long-range accuracy of infantry rifles, so the carbine seemed the obvious answer. Artillery carbines were also routinely issued to garrison troops manning fixed fortifications.

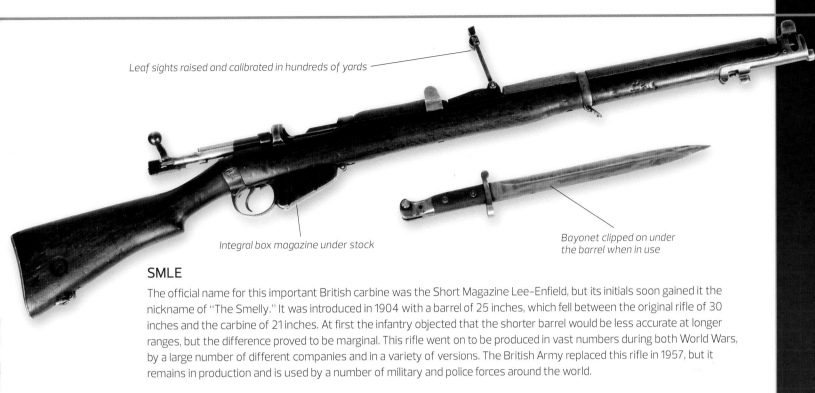

Leaf sights raised and calibrated in hundreds of yards

Integral box magazine under stock

Bayonet clipped on under the barrel when in use

SMLE

The official name for this important British carbine was the Short Magazine Lee–Enfield, but its initials soon gained it the nickname of "The Smelly." It was introduced in 1904 with a barrel of 25 inches, which fell between the original rifle of 30 inches and the carbine of 21 inches. At first the infantry objected that the shorter barrel would be less accurate at longer ranges, but the difference proved to be marginal. This rifle went on to be produced in vast numbers during both World Wars, by a large number of different companies and in a variety of versions. The British Army replaced this rifle in 1957, but it remains in production and is used by a number of military and police forces around the world.

BATTLE OF THE LITTLE BIG HORN

General George Armstrong Custer and his Michigan Cavalry made effective use of the Spencer carbine at the Battle of Hanover, fought on June 30, 1863, as part of the Gettysburg Campaign. The massed volleys of the repeating carbines drove off an attack by Confederate Jeb Stuart and effectively turned the tide of battle. At the Battle of the Little Big Horn in 1876, Custer again relied on the firepower of his men's carbines, this time against the Lakota, Cheyenne, and Arapaho tribes. However, Custer's 7th Cavalry was equipped with the Springfield Model 1873 carbine. This weapon was robust and weatherproof, but subsequent tests showed that after prolonged firing the hot barrel caused the copper cartridges to expand and jam. It is now thought that this jamming of the carbines contributed to the total annihilation of Custer's command.

VETTERLI ARTILLERY

A Model 1871 Vetterli artillery carbine. This gun is very similar to the Model 1871 cavalry carbine, having a similar action and barrel. The magazine of these Swiss-designed, but Italian-made guns was based on that of the American Winchester 1866, while the bolt action was derived from the German *Dreyse* rifle. This particular model is a single-shot weapon, the magazine being discarded. The advantages of a repeating rifle were not considered necessary for the gunners and garrison troops to which this gun was issued.

Leaf sight fitted further forward than usual, reducing accuracy of aim

Bolt-action breech

Wooden stock with fitting for shoulder sling

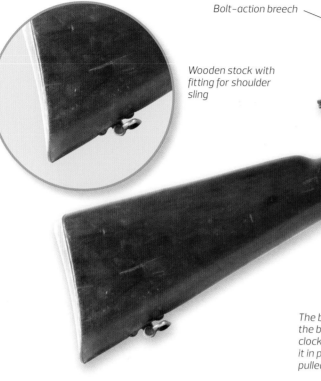

The bolt action of the Vetterli required the bolt to be rotated 90 degrees anti-clockwise to unlock the lugs that held it in position before the bolt could be pulled back to open the breech.

UHLANS

During the Napoleonic Wars, Polish light cavalry named *uhlans* proved to be especially effective. Their distinctive weapons and dashing uniforms made them popular additions to other armies and soon most countries had regiments of uhlans. Uhlan regiments were equipped with lances, carbines, and sabres, while their uniforms featured the square-topped *Czapka* helmet and a colorful plastron over the chest and a sash around the waist. The lance gave the initial charge of the uhlan greater shock power as it outreached enemy sabres, but was then discarded as the weapon was unwieldy in close combat.

The name "Uhlan" comes from the Polish nobleman of Tatar extraction Alexander Uhlan who raised and commanded a regiment of Tatar horsemen to serve in the Polish army during the first quarter of the 18th century. His regiment became known as "Uhlan's Children" and continued to serve the Polish kings after his death. In 1914 the Germans, Austrians and Russians all employed uhlans extensively to rove ahead of the infantry, using their carbines to harass enemy troops. The British also had lance-armed troops in 1914, but they were called simply "lancers" and lacked the more flamboyant elements of Uhlan outfits.

Open metal fore sight led to complaints of inaccuracy if heavy usage on campaign caused the metal to become bent.

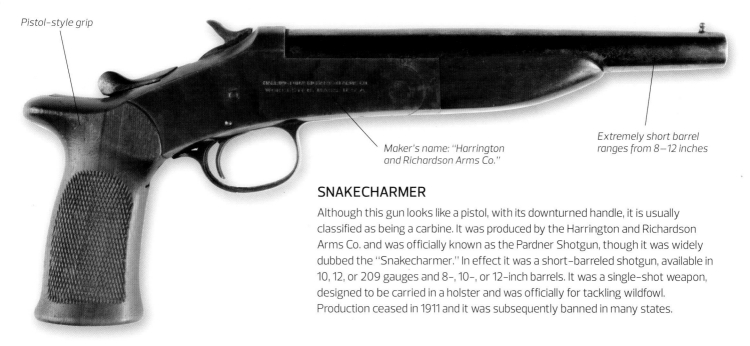

Pistol-style grip

Maker's name: "Harrington and Richardson Arms Co."

Extremely short barrel ranges from 8–12 inches

SNAKECHARMER

Although this gun looks like a pistol, with its downturned handle, it is usually classified as being a carbine. It was produced by the Harrington and Richardson Arms Co. and was officially known as the Pardner Shotgun, though it was widely dubbed the "Snakecharmer." In effect it was a short-barreled shotgun, available in 10, 12, or 209 gauges and 8-, 10-, or 12-inch barrels. It was a single-shot weapon, designed to be carried in a holster and was officially for tackling wildfowl. Production ceased in 1911 and it was subsequently banned in many states.

The lock of this Baker Rifle uses a percussion cap, indicating that it was manufactured after 1830 by which time production of this rifle was falling. It can be difficult to distinguish between the small number of Bakers produced with a percussion-cap system and those that began life as flintlocks and were changed later.

Barrel contains 7 rectangular grooves

Straight-style shoulder stock. Some models had a bent stock

BAKER RIFLE

Widely known as the Baker Rifle after its designer Ezekiel Baker, the first rifle to be widely used in the British Army was officially the Pattern 1800 Infantry Rifle. It fired a lead ball 0.6 inches in diameter and was accurate enough to reliably hit a man at 200 yards, making it far more accurate than contemporary muskets. The accuracy was paid for by a rate of fire about half that of a musket.

Modern Carbines

While traditional carbines were produced for cavalrymen, more modern carbines have a wider range of uses and users. In the military, they are provided to truck drivers, tank crews, or others who would find a full-size rifle too much of a handful.

In civilian use they have a similarly diverse range of uses. Many hunters moving through forest find a long rifle snags on undergrowth too often for comfort, and prefer a shorter weapon even if there is a loss of long range accuracy.

Rear sight (users said it was inaccurate)

Metal jacket around barrel protects hand from barrel heat

Magazine holding 6 rounds

Metal shoulder-stock plate

THE GRENADIER

Officially this combination weapon is the *Moschetto per Truppe Speciali con Tromboncino Modele 91/28*, but it was generally called "the grenadier." It is a standard Carcano Modele 1891 carbine, with the new 17-inch barrel introduced in 1928, but it has had a 38.5mm grenade launcher attached to the side of the barrel. It was designed to be used by elite units in the Italian army, including the Alpine infantry. By the outbreak of World War II, the Italian Army was in the process of re-equipping with a new rifle, the Model 1938, but only a few units were re-equipped. The Modele 91/28 carbines were taken out of service in the 1950s, but large numbers remain in private hands.

Magazine holding 10 rounds

SKS CARBINE

One of the most numerous guns ever made, it is thought that over 15 million examples of the SKS Carbine and its variants have been produced. It is a self-loading, light-weight weapon designed to be used by support troops, though it did see service in the front line during World War II. The SKS was designed in the Soviet Union in 1943 to be produced in vast numbers and to be used by the poorly trained infantry being pushed into battle as the German penetration of Russia reached its height. The ability to withstand rain, snow, ice and mud was paramount, as was ease of maintenance. The entire gun can be stripped for cleaning and reassembled without needing any tools at all.

Folding metal stock

Pistol-style grip

Curved 30-round magazine

M1 CARBINE

The American M1 Carbine was produced in 1941 by Winchester in response to a demand from the US Army for what was then called a "light rifle." At this date all troops other than front-line infantry were given pistols. The idea now was to arm truck drivers, gunners, tank crews, and other support personnel with something that had more hitting power than a pistol, but easier to carry about than the heavy infantry rifle. A new ammunition, the .30 carbine was introduced with a lighter construction and reduced propellant. The resulting weapon weighed just over 5lb, had a barrel of 18 inches, and carried a 15-round magazine. The weapon proved to be highly effective in its intended role, greatly increasing the firepower available to second-line troops. When issued to front-line units, however, it proved to be too delicate to stand up to tough campaign conditions.

Bayonet stored under barrel, but hinges forward when needed

Ring sight

MERRILL'S MARAUDERS

The World War II American unit officially named the 5307th Composite Unit (Provisional) was almost universally known as "Merrill's Marauders" after its commander Frank Merrill. The unit was formed in 1943 as a light-infantry unit tasked with penetrating deep behind Japanese lines to attack supply lines, depots, and other targets. Operating up to 1,000 miles behind enemy lines in Burma and China, the Marauders used mules for transport in remote areas and were supplied by air. Because weight was always an issue, the troops were equipped with the M1 carbine, which proved to be highly effective in the close-range combat of jungle fighting, though prone to fall victim to rough handling.

Frank Merrill (left) and General Joseph Stilwell in Burma.

The World Wars

Global Conflicts

The 20th century was an age of global conflicts like no other century the world had seen. Twice the globe erupted into a conflict that reached to every corner of the world, from Arctic frozen lands to the steamiest of jungles, from remote islands to massive cities. The weapons that the men who fought in these wars used had to be able to cope with not only the enemy, but also with a range of conditions that earlier weapons had not encountered. And the face of battle was changing rapidly as well. The rifles with which men marched to war in 1914 were very different from those being introduced in 1945.

IN 1954 the Communist regime in Bulgaria erected a huge monument to the Red Army in gratitude to the Soviet Union for having liberated the country from the Germans. Many non-Communists have long resented the triumphalist Communist monument and since the return of democracy the monument has been regularly vandalized and repaired. There is now a growing movement to have the monument demolished, while others want it preserved as a reminder of the evils of Communism.

Austria-Hungary

The Austro-Hungarian Empire that initiated World War I by declaring war on Serbia on July 28, 1914, was one of the oldest political units in the world, but was doomed to be destroyed by the war it had begun. The ruling Habsburg Dynasty had been founded by Radbog von Habsburg when he obtained the title of Count from the Holy Roman Emperor in 1020. The Habsurgs had gone on to become one of the most powerful families in the world. In 1914 they ruled an empire that included a vast area of central-southern Europe. After defeat in 1918 the empire broke up to form Austria, Hungary, and Czechoslovakia, with parts of the empire going to Poland, Romania, Yugoslavia, and Italy. The weapons that the empire took to war in 1914 served as the models for the armies of the successor states.

Magazine holding 5 cartridges

Bayonet blade faces upward when fixed

STEYR-MANNLICHER

A *Steyr-Mannlicher* Model 1895 Rifle made in Austria for the Habsburg Army during World War I. The rifle used a highly unusual bolt action that required the rifleman to jerk it straight back, rather than twist it backward as in most other rifles. This resulted in a very high rate of fire—up to 35 rounds per minute in test conditions—but could lead to problems with jamming in dirty campaign conditions. The Habsburgs bought about 3 million of these rifles themselves, and sold large numbers to allies such as Bulgaria and Turkey. It remained in service with the Hungarian and Bulgarian armies throughout World War II.

BAYONET

The unusual bayonet made for the Steyr-Mannlicher Model 1895. The wooden-handled blade could be used as a multi-purpose knife on campaign, but what really made it unusual was that when fitted to the rifle, the sharp edge pointed upward, unlike every other bayonet in the world at that time. This model of bayonet was made in a number of factories throughout the Habsburg Empire and there are many differences of detail.

Ring sight

CZECH MAUSER

Magazine holds 5 rounds

The German Mauser company produced a wide range of sporting and military rifles in the 19th century, but it was the Model 98 that made it internationally famous. The repeating bolt-action rifle had a 5-round magazine with a smooth, robust action. This is a VZ24 Rifle, made in Czechoslovakia in 1924. Despite its name, this is effectively a Mauser 98 with a shorter barrel. When Germany invaded Czechoslovakia in 1939 these rifles were taken for use by the German Army and proved to be so similar to the German rifle that no changes in training or equipment were needed.

SIEGE OF PRZEMYSL

The Austro-Hungarian Army was not highly regarded in 1914. However, its likely adversaries were either small, for instance the Serb Army, or of even poorer quality, notably the Russian Army. The Austro-Hungarian reputation gained a major boost in September 1914 at the Siege of Przemysl. In August 1914 the Russians advanced across the open country of Galicia, the Austro-Hungarians falling back to the more easily defended Carpathian Mountains. The fortified city of Przemysl blocked roads and the River San from being used for Russian supplies. It was garrisoned by 120,000 Habsburg infantry armed with Steyr-Mannlicher rifles. The initial Russian assault was thrown back with 40,000 casualties, but little loss to the defenders. The Russians thereafter generally stayed out of range of the Steyr-Mannlichers. The defenders were finally forced to surrender after 133 days when they ran out of food.

Belgium

Belgium joined both World Wars when it was invaded by Germany. In 1914 the Belgian army was 117,000 strong, plus large numbers of reservists. It was well-trained but generally lacked heavy weaponry and relied heavily on fortified strongpoints to resist invasion. In 1940 the army was larger, but still lacked heavy weapons and again relied largely on static defenses to slow down a German offensive until the much larger French Army could come to Belgium's defense. Belgium had an active armaments industry, but this concentrated on small arms.

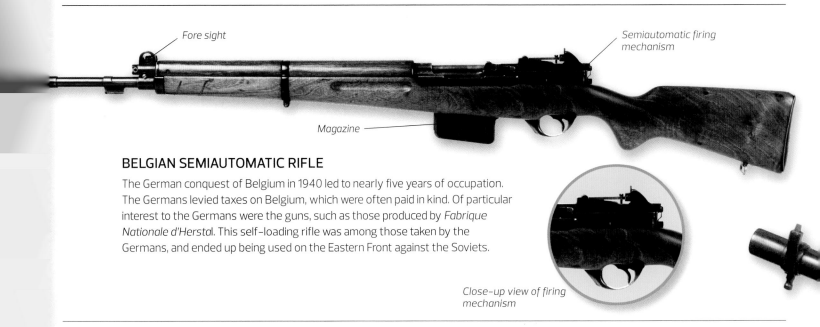

Fore sight

Semiautomatic firing mechanism

Magazine

BELGIAN SEMIAUTOMATIC RIFLE

The German conquest of Belgium in 1940 led to nearly five years of occupation. The Germans levied taxes on Belgium, which were often paid in kind. Of particular interest to the Germans were the guns, such as those produced by *Fabrique Nationale d'Herstal*. This self-loading rifle was among those taken by the Germans, and ended up being used on the Eastern Front against the Soviets.

Close-up view of firing mechanism

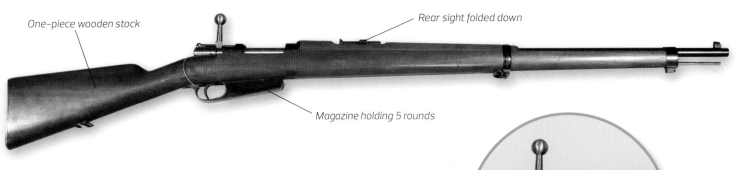

One-piece wooden stock

Rear sight folded down

Magazine holding 5 rounds

MAUSER MODEL 89 CAVALRY CARBINE

In 1887 the Belgian King Leopold II and his government decided that the country's armed forces required modernization. After a good deal of thought a specification for a new rifle was drawn up, but rather than ask manufacturers to submit designs the Belgians looked around for the rifle already in production that was nearest to what they wanted. They chose the Mauser Model 71/84 and in return for a large order Mauser agreed to make some changes. These were principally the development of a stripper clip to feed ammunition into the magazine, increasing the rate of fire, and the fitting of a barrel shroud to protect the barrel from rough handling on campaign. The result was the Mauser 89 Belgian, produced in both an infantry rifle and cavalry carbine version. It was this gun that the Belgians used in World War I.

The Belgian Mauser carbine used the same Mauser bolt action as the earlier Model 71/84 Rifle

EBEN EMAEL

In 1931 Belgian strategists believed that any future German invasion would come across the Albert Canal at Eben-Emael, near Maastrictht. They therefore constructed a massive fortress where the canal passed through a deep cutting. The fort was built of reinforced concrete, thick enough to withstand the heaviest artillery in the world, and equipped with 120mm and 75mm artillery plus machine-gun posts. It was considered impregnable. On May 10, 1940, 78 German paratroopers landed on top of the fort using gliders. They began placing demolition charges that destroyed the fort's guns and bunkers one by one. Lacking rifles or carbines, the defenders were unable to climb on to the roof and attack the paratroopers. After much of the fort had been destroyed, the defenders surrendered.

HOTCHKISS M1909 MACHINE GUN

In 1909 the French company *Hotchkiss et Cie* produced a new light machine gun. It was quickly adopted by the Belgian army and bought in large numbers. The gun was gas-operated and water-cooled, firing bullets from either a strip feed or a belt feed. It could fire up to 400 rounds per minute and had a maximum range of 4,000 yards, though it was accurate at much less than that. The light weight of the gun, only 25lb, made it acceptable for cavalry use as it could be carried intact, with ammunition on other horses, and brought into action very quickly if the horsemen encountered opposition.

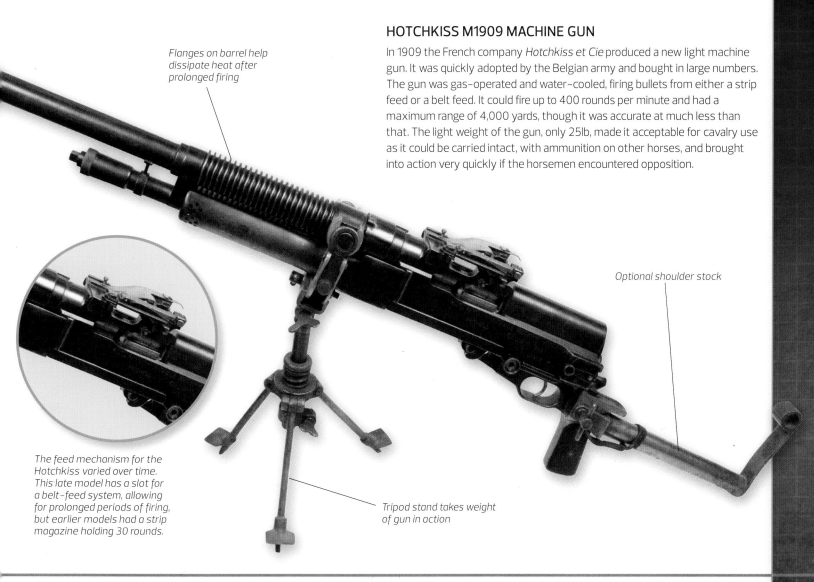

Flanges on barrel help dissipate heat after prolonged firing

Optional shoulder stock

The feed mechanism for the Hotchkiss varied over time. This late model has a slot for a belt-feed system, allowing for prolonged periods of firing, but earlier models had a strip magazine holding 30 rounds.

Tripod stand takes weight of gun in action

Britain and the British Empire

Britain entered World War I with an army that was small by continental standards and that was equipped and trained largely to deal with conflicts in the colonies. Those conflicts tended to be against opponents who were poorly equipped, but who operated with the advantages of difficult terrain and simple logistical needs. As a result the British Army came equipped with cavalry, mobile light artillery, and infantry equipped with long-range rifles, while all the men were trained to use their initiative and adopt flexible tactics. The British equipment had been chosen with an eye to being used in desert, jungle, or mountains and so was generally robust and easily maintained. Faced by large-scale armies operating over a European landscape, the British Army was forced to learn fast lessons in terms of tactics and weaponry.

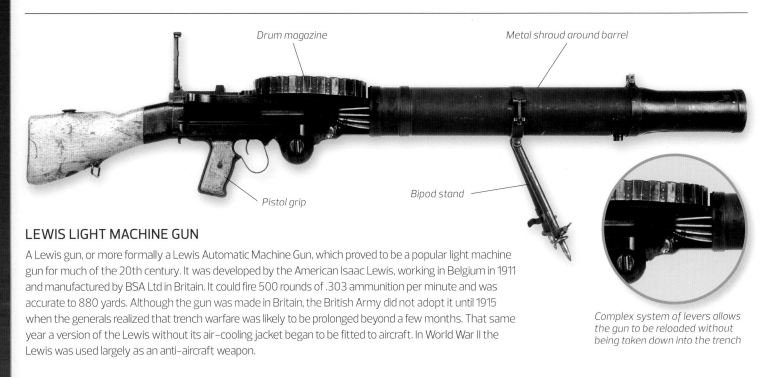

Drum magazine

Metal shroud around barrel

Pistol grip

Bipod stand

Complex system of levers allows the gun to be reloaded without being taken down into the trench

LEWIS LIGHT MACHINE GUN

A Lewis gun, or more formally a Lewis Automatic Machine Gun, which proved to be a popular light machine gun for much of the 20th century. It was developed by the American Isaac Lewis, working in Belgium in 1911 and manufactured by BSA Ltd in Britain. It could fire 500 rounds of .303 ammunition per minute and was accurate to 880 yards. Although the gun was made in Britain, the British Army did not adopt it until 1915 when the generals realized that trench warfare was likely to be prolonged beyond a few months. That same year a version of the Lewis without its air-cooling jacket began to be fitted to aircraft. In World War II the Lewis was used largely as an anti-aircraft weapon.

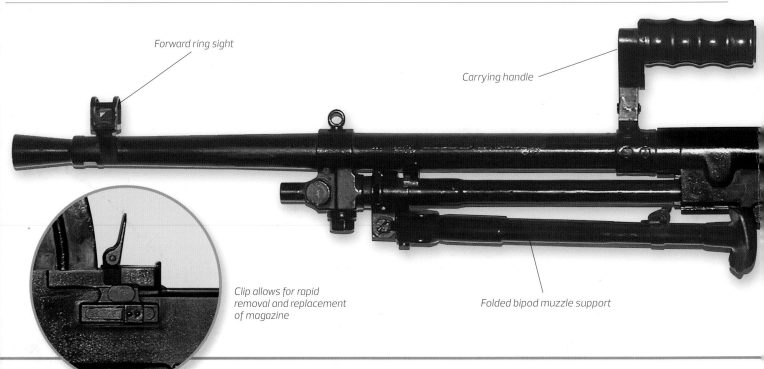

Forward ring sight

Carrying handle

Clip allows for rapid removal and replacement of magazine

Folded bipod muzzle support

OLD CONTEMPTIBLES

In 1914 Britain sent an army of six infantry and one cavalry division to assist the Belgians and French in fighting the German invading army. Compared to the vast French and German armies of around 1.5 million men each, the British force was small. On August 19, 1914, Germany's Kaiser Wilhelm II issued an order that is usually translated, but not entirely accurately, as reading "exterminate the treacherous English and walk over this contemptible little army." The British were thrown into the arduous Retreat from Mons and suffered heavy casualties, but they stopped the German advance. The survivors of the campaign thereafter referred to themselves as "Old Contemptibles." By 1915 the large mass of new volunteers began to arrive in France, with the Old Contemptibles usually raised to the rank of corporal or sergeant and tasked with training the new arrivals in modern warfare.

"A" Company of the 4th Battalion, Royal Fusiliers (9th Brigade, 3rd Division) on 22 August, 1914, resting in the square at Mons, Belgium, the day before the Battle of Mons. Minutes after this photo was taken the company moved into position at Nimy on the bank of the Mons–Condé Canal.

VICKERS–BERTHIER LIGHT MACHINE GUN

A Vickers–Berthier light machine gun. The Vickers–Berthier began life as a light machine gun designed by Frenchman Adolphe Berthier in 1913, but this was not a commercial success. In 1925 the British Vickers company bought the design and introduced a number of improvements with the hope that it would be adopted by the British Army as its new light machine gun. In the event that contract was awarded to the Bren gun, which was lighter and shorter. However, the Indian Army preferred the cheaper Vickers Berthier, which was easier to maintain in the field. Large numbers were manufactured at the Ishapore Factory, and it is believed that they remain in storage as a reserve weapon for the Indian Army.

Box magazine has curved shape due to shape of standard British ammunition

Rear leaf sights raised for firing

Butt shaped to fit comfortably into the shoulder

Mirror

Complex system of levers allows the gun to be reloaded without being taken down into the trench

Mirror

Trigger

PERISCOPE RIFLE

A Lee-Enfield rifle adapted to be a Periscope rifle that could be pushed over the parapet of a trench and fired by a man sitting inside the trench and peering through the attached mirrors. This is a later model with purpose-built metal fittings and linkages. The original periscope rifle was invented by Sergeant William Beech of the 2nd Battalion of the Australian Imperial Force when he was serving in the trenches of Gallipoli in 1915. Beech's version was rather more ad hoc than the weapon seen here, utilizing bits of wood, pieces of string, and a shaving mirror to produce the desired effect.

BAYONET NO.4 MKII

The Bayonet No.4 MkII bayonet was the standard British bayonet in the later stages of World War II, and was widely used by colonial and Commonwealth forces. The Pattern 1907 bayonet had seen Britain through World War I, but it was felt that a lighter bayonet was needed. The Bayonet No.4 was introduced in 1939 with a distinctive cruciform cross-section, but it proved to be difficult to mass produce so the MkII with a simpler socket was introduced. The weapon was produced in the factories of the Singer Sewing Machine company, pressed into war work for the duration.

The "spike" design means the bayonet is sharpened only at its point

Aperture for belt-feed ammunition

Jacket contains water pipes to cool barrel

COLT–VICKERS MACHINE GUN

The Vickers Machine Gun was the standard British infantry machine gun, remaining in service through to 1968. The gun was extremely rugged and reliable, able to fire continuously for hours on end without jamming, so long as there was enough water to operate the cooling system. The gun could fire 450 rounds of .303 ammunition per minute and was accurate to well over a mile. The only real drawback to the Vickers as a weapon was its weight. The gun required a crew of eight, only two of whom operated the weapon in action while the rest were needed to carry the gun, ammunition, spare parts and water. This example is the American-built Colt–Vickers.

Cocking handle

Side-mounted box magazine

Breech block operates on blow-back open-breech principle

Rifle-style stock

STEN GUN

Nearly five million Sten Guns were produced, largely because they were cheap to make and simple to use. It could fire up to 500 rounds of 9mm ammunition per minute from a detachable 32-round magazine. The design proved to be so straightforward to manufacture that dozens of unauthorized versions have been produced around the world to equip insurgent and terrorist groups. Set against these advantages was the fact that it was very prone to jamming and was inaccurate at ranges over 100 yards, and often less than that.

BATTLE OF LOOS

The Battle of Loos was a British offensive against the Germans on the Western Front that began on September 25, 1915, and ended on October 14. The initial British attack was a success, breaking the German lines and reaching the open ground beyond. However, muddled orders and a failure to bring up reserves in time, plus a swift German response, meant that the success could not be exploited before the Germans closed the gap. The nature of fighting showed the more perceptive officers on both sides that the traditional infantry rifle, with its long range accuracy, was wholly unsuited to trench warfare.

British infantry from the 47th (1/2nd London) Division advancing into a gas cloud during the Battle of Loos.

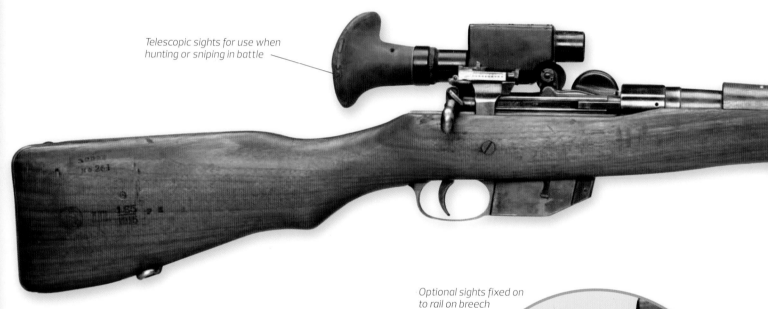

Telescopic sights for use when hunting or sniping in battle

Optional sights fixed on to rail on breech

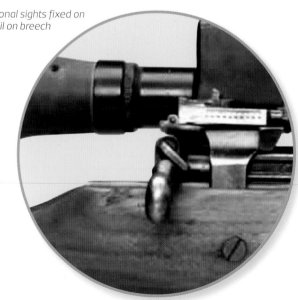

ROSS RIFLE

The Canadian Ross Rifle was a weapon that entered military service with great hopes, but proved to be a disaster and had to be rapidly withdrawn. The MkI of 1903 and the MkII of 1905 were both excellent sporting and target rifles, which were both accurate and reliable. The Royal Northwest Mounted Police—the famous "Mounties"—adopted the MkII and by 1908 had made a number of recommendations on how the rifle could be improved for use in the field. These were adopted and the MkIII was produced in 1910. The Canadian government, eager to have a home-produced weapon for its army, bought the Ross MkIII in large numbers. When Canadian soldiers entered the trenches of the Western Front they soon found that the mud could easily get into the bolt mechanism and cause a jam. This, combined with the fact that the bayonet would fall off when the gun was fired, caused the weapon to be withdrawn from service.

BREN GUN

The Bren Gun was the standard British infantry machine gun in World War II, remaining in service until 2006 and still in use with the Indian Army. The Bren began life in 1935 as the Czech ZBvs.26, but was adapted by the British to take the standard British .303 ammunition. The name comes from the initial two letters of Brno, where it was designed, and Enfield, where it was made. The gas-operated, air-cooled gun can fire 500 rounds a minute and is accurate to 600 yards, with a maximum range of 1,850 yards. Although generally fired form a bipod support, the Bren also had a canvas shoulder sling to allow it to be fired from a standing position.

Carrying handle

Rear sight

Bipod muzzle support

Metal butt plate was fitted to MkII and later models

Ring fore sight

Fore sight

Barrel 25.2 inches long

Magazine holds 10 rounds

The distinctive snub snout of the SMLE. The small protruding knob beneath the muzzle is the bayonet boss, while the iron sights above are stepped slightly back from the muzzle.

SMLE LEE-ENFIELD MKIII

By 1915 the demands of trench warfare on a large scale were starting to have an impact on the British military. The basic SMLE Lee-Enfield was found to be so complex that it could not be reliably manufactured by the many non-military factories being pressed into the war effort. Moreover its great accuracy was not really needed in the cramped conditions of trench warfare. The result was the MkIII that entered service in 1915. This weapon had a simplified magazine and less complex cocking mechanism as well as more functional sights.

Tall fore sight

Barrel could be removed for cleaning

Detachable 10-round magazine

LEE-METFORD

The Lee-Metford was an older infantry rifle that had been officially phased out when World War I began, though it was still in use for target shooting and some saw active service. The rifle was a marriage between the bolt action invented by James Lee and the barrel of William Metford, both considered the finest of their day. Lee's bolt needed only a 60-degree twist and was placed over the trigger, making it faster to operate than contemporary systems. Metford's rifling had a smooth, rounded profile, very different from the conventional squared grooves. The rifle entered service in 1888, but when smokeless powder was introduced it was found the more powerful propellant stripped Metford's rifling after just 5,000 rounds.

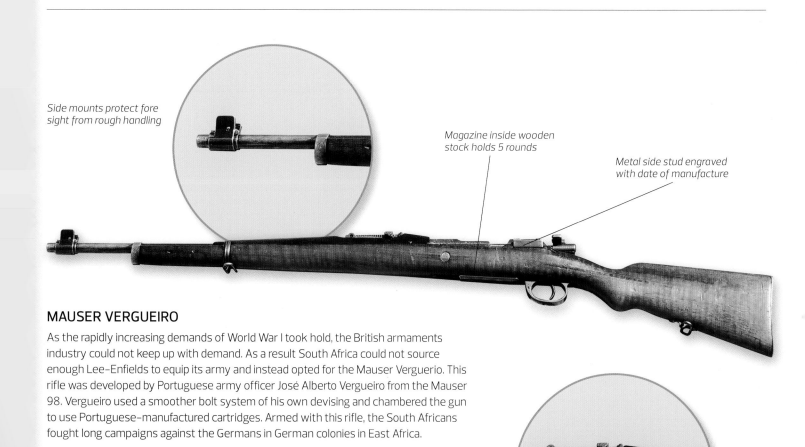

Side mounts protect fore sight from rough handling

Magazine inside wooden stock holds 5 rounds

Metal side stud engraved with date of manufacture

MAUSER VERGUEIRO

As the rapidly increasing demands of World War I took hold, the British armaments industry could not keep up with demand. As a result South Africa could not source enough Lee-Enfields to equip its army and instead opted for the Mauser Verguerio. This rifle was developed by Portuguese army officer José Alberto Vergueiro from the Mauser 98. Vergueiro used a smoother bolt system of his own devising and chambered the gun to use Portuguese-manufactured cartridges. Armed with this rifle, the South Africans fought long campaigns against the Germans in German colonies in East Africa.

The iron sights were typical of the period, but the leaf sights when raised were marked in 100-meter steps from 200 to 2,000 meters, although it was generally held to be accurate to only about 1,000 meters.

D-DAY

On June 6, 1944, the Allies launched a massive invasion of German-occupied France that saw 160,000 soldiers storm ashore in less than 24 hours, followed by tens of thousands more over the days that followed. Most of the infantry involved carried rifles and light machine guns not very dissimilar to those used in World War I, however specialist troops carried a wider variety of small arms. Many of the paratroops, for instance, were equipped with automatic or semiautomatic weapons.

A LCVP (Landing Craft, Vehicle, Personnel) from the U.S. Coast Guard-manned USS Samuel Chase disembarks troops of Company E, 16th Infantry, 1st Infantry Division (the Big Red One) wading onto the Fox Green section of Omaha Beach (Calvados, Basse-Normandie, France) on the morning of June 6, 1944. American soldiers encountered the newly formed German 352nd Division when landing. During the initial landing two-thirds of the Company E became casualties.

China

China played only a small part in World War I due to internal problems, nor was China inclined to join either of the warring sides having fought campaigns against the German, British, French, and Russians within living memory. The last emperor was forced to abdicate in 1912. The subsequent Republic collapsed in 1916 as regional military commanders seized local power and ushered in a decade of civil war that became known as the Warlord Era. By 1927 southern and central China had been unified under the *Kuomintang* Movement, while northern warlords sought a peace settlement that gave them some measure of independence. The Communists, meanwhile, held out at Shaanxi. Into this troubled, confusing picture marched the Japanese army in 1931 claiming to be acting in the name of the dethroned emperor, who was set up as a puppet ruler in Japanese occupied areas. When Japan attacked the USA and Britain, China was accepted as one of the Allies and so her war against Japan became part of the wider World War II.

Barrel length 514mm

Three piece wooden stock

Magazine holds 5 rounds

MOSIN-NAGANT M1891 CAVALRY CARBINE

The Chinese stocks of this Russian carbine had come from a variety of sources. Some were bought before World War I, others found their way south during the Russian civil war and still others were given to China by Japan from stocks captured in the 1904 Russo-Japanese War.

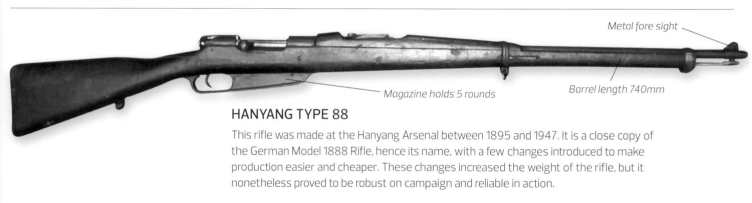

Metal fore sight

Magazine holds 5 rounds

Barrel length 740mm

HANYANG TYPE 88

This rifle was made at the Hanyang Arsenal between 1895 and 1947. It is a close copy of the German Model 1888 Rifle, hence its name, with a few changes introduced to make production easier and cheaper. These changes increased the weight of the rifle, but it nonetheless proved to be robust on campaign and reliable in action.

Mauser bolt action

Barrel length 590mm

The breech is chambered to take the 7x57mm Mauser cartridge

VZ24

The VZ24 was a rifle produced in Czechoslovakia from the famous Mauser 98 design, but with a shorter barrel and some minor changes. The weapon was designed for the export market and was produced in huge numbers throughout the 1920s and 1930s. The weapon was sold to the Kuomintang, but captured weapons ended up in the hands of various warlord armies and were used by the Communists.

BATTLE OF TAIERZHUANG

The Battle of Taierzhuang in 1938 was a rare Chinese victory in the Sino-Japanese War. The campaign began with a Japanese advance on the large city of Xuzhou, but attacks by Chinese guerillas on their supply lines forced the Japanese to halt at Taierzhuang to regroup. An attack on the town walls of Taierzhuang on March 29 was halted by Chinese rifle fire, as was a second assault a week later. On April 6 the Japanese, short on food and ammunition, were forced to retreat. The withdrawal became a rout, but the Chinese lacked modern transport to capitalize fully on the victory they had won by determined rifle fire from strong defensive positions. Even so the Chinese captured 1,000 machine guns and 10,000 rifles from the fleeing Japanese.

Ring fore sight

Magazine holding 20 rounds

The aluminum forend was ribbed and served as a heat dissipater to cool the barrel during prolonged firing. Ironically it was the weapon's vulnerability to malfunction at low temperatures the caused it to be distrusted by front-line troops.

ZH29

The ZH29 was the first successful semiautomatic rifle to enter service with a national army. It was designed in Czechoslovakia in 1929 by Emanuel Holek who used the gas exhaust from the cartridge to operate a reloading mechanism. It was bought in numbers by the Kuomintang.

The folding rear sight was located behind the breech. This was usually considered impractical in a bolt-action rifle, but was possible in this self-loading weapon.

SVT38

In 1935 Soviet dictator Josef Stalin ordered that trials be held for a semiautomatic rifle with a view to re-equipping the Red Army. The contest was won by the SVT38, which had an impressive performance. Stalin then ordered that shipments of the new gun be sent to the Chinese Communists, fighting a war against both the Japanese and other Chinese factions.

Baffled muzzle break helps contend with recoil

Wooden stock with fitting for sling

10-round magazine

Finland

Throughout most of the 19th century, Finland was a nominally independent Grand Duchy, although the Grand Duke of Finland was the same person as the Tsar of Russia. When the Tsar abdicated in 1917 the Finns took the opportunity to declare themselves an independent republic. The new Communist government in Russia resented the loss of Finland and in November 1939 launched an unprovoked invasion. The resulting Winter War saw the Finns inflict serious defeats on the Red Army, but they were eventually overwhelmed by the vast numbers of men the Russians sent in. The peace treaty gave Russia large stretches of border lands. When Germany invaded Russia in 1941, the Finns joined in with the aim of recovering the lost border territory. Finland made a separate peace in 1944, again losing its border lands but retaining its democratic government and trade links to the West.

Rear sight folded down

Bayonet

Trigger and guard

MOSIN–NAGANT M28

The M28 was a version of the reliable Mosin–Nagant 1891 that was made in Finland using barrels manufactured in Germany by SIG. Apart from some minor design changes to the trigger and trigger guard, it was identical to the M27 carbine version of the M1891 that featured a shorter but more robust barrel than the Russian original.

BATTLE OF THE RAATE ROAD

Fought in January 1940 as the Russian Red Army invaded Finland, the Raate Road was a decisive defeat for the Russians that effectively ended the first phase of the war. In December 1939 the Russians had captured Suomussalmi, but the Finns then cut the Raate Road, the main supply route from Russia to Suomussalmi. On January 1 the Russian 44th Division under Alexey Vinogradov set out to reopen the route. The Finns used their "motti" tactics to keep the road blocked. Motti saw the Finnish troops moving rapidly through the wooded landscape in dispersed formations before concentrating to achieve a local numerical superiority over a unit of the Red Army. A short battle would then be fought to annihilate the Russians, after which the Finns melted back into the trackless forests. After seven days and nights of motti, the 15,000-strong 44th Division was reduced to just 6,000 men and had lost all its vehicles. The Finns had lost only 402 men. When he heard of the disaster Stalin had Vinogradov shot, along with his senior subordinates.

LAHTI–SALORANTA M26

Every platoon in the Finnish Army included two M26 machine guns, each with a two-man crew. The gun had a 20-round magazine and could fire 450 rounds per minute over 500 yards. The weapon was used to put down covering fire as the infantry moved from one position to the next.

Monopod muzzle support

Box magazine containing 20 rounds

The pistol grip was designed to be used by men wearing thick gloves which, together with the internal oiling system, made this a reliable weapon even in Finnish winter conditions.

Barrel length 540mm

CARCANO 1891

The Carcano 1891 was the standard bolt–action rifle of the Italian army in World War I. In 1938 the Italian government began to replace its Carcano's with the new Modello 1938 that had a larger caliber and shorter barrel. As the Carcano rifles were taken out of service they were put up for sale, with Finland buying as many as it could get.

Magazine holds 6 rounds

PPSH–41

The Soviet PPSh–41 submachine gun was highly regarded by the Finnish army, and was put to use whenever examples could be captured. Ironically it was the disasters suffered by the Red Army in Finland in 1939–40 that spurred the development of a submachine gun that could be used to spray bullets at close ranges. The PPSh–41 entered production in 1941, but it was not until 1943 that it was being mass manufactured. It could fire over 900 rounds per minute from a 71-round drum magazine and was accurate to about 150 yards.

Drum magazine holds 71 rounds

Metal shroud around barrel

Barrel length 269mm

France

In both 1914 and 1939 France had a large army of mostly conscripts and reservists recalled to duty when war broke out. In 1914, the French high command expected to fight a war of open movement and were confident of success. Their 75mm Model 1897 cannon was the most modern in the world, while their infantry were armed with modern rifles. In the event, they fought a grinding trench campaign. French commanders in 1940 expected to fight a trench campaign, argued with each other, and were generally despondent about their chances. Again they had modern weapons, including tanks and aircraft, though the French infantry had equipment very similar to that of 1914. In fact, they faced a highly mobile campaign, and lost disastrously.

FRENCH CHAUCHAT

Officially the *Fusil Mitrailleuse Mle 1915 CSRG*, the standard light machine gun of the French Army in both World Wars was more usually known as the *Chauchat* after its inventor, Colonel Louis Chauchat. The weapon could fire 240 rounds per minute and was considered to be accurate to 200 yards, though its maximum range was given as 2,200 yards. Although it was an effective weapon in ideal conditions, the Chauchat suffered in the trenches because mud and grit could easily enter the magazines and so cause it to jam.

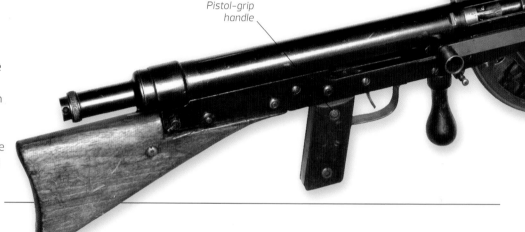

Pistol-grip handle

HOTCHKISS M1909 MACHINE GUN

The Hotchkiss M1909 was the version of this versatile machine gun used by the French Army, other models being used by the British, Belgian and US Armies. Compared to other machine guns of this date, the M1909 was relatively light and easily dismantled for transport on horseback. As a result it was used by the Australian Light Horse and New Zealand Mounted Rifles during the campaigns in Palestine and Sinai in 1915 to 1917. It was also used by the US Army in its Mexican Expedition of 1916 to 1917. The only real flaw of this gun was the fact that it was easy to push the magazine in upside down, thus causing a jam, especially at night.

Detachable metal shoulder stock

Flanged barrel sleeve

Ball swivel mount

Barrel sleeve

Flared muzzle

Bipod muzzle support

Magazine

BATTLE OF BROODESIENDE

The Battle of Broodseinde was fought on October 4, 1917, near Ypres in Flanders, by the British Second and Fifth armies against the German Fourth Army. Using "bite-and-hold" tactics, with objectives limited to what could be held against German counter-attacks, the British devastated the German defense, which prompted a crisis among the German commanders and caused a severe loss of morale in the German Fourth Army. It was the most successful Allied attack of the Battle of Passchendaele.

FRENCH MAS

The MAS-38 was a French submachine gun that entered service in 1938, though it had been designed 15 years earlier. It could fire 600 rounds per minute from its 32-round box magazine and was accurate to about 150 yards. The unusual bulge in the wooden stock is to house the bolt-recoil system. The MAS-38 was a high-quality weapon built to exacting standards. When France surrendered to Germany in 1940 the Germans not only took all existing MAS-38s for their own use, but also continued production up to 1944. As a result more of these French weapons saw service with the German Army than with the French.

The distinctive bulge in the shoulder stock contains a metal tube along which the bolt recoils when the gun is fired

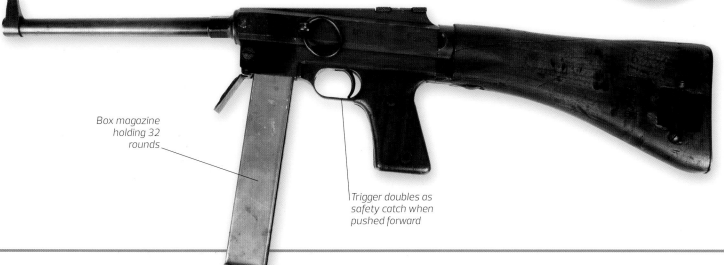

Box magazine holding 32 rounds

Trigger doubles as safety catch when pushed forward

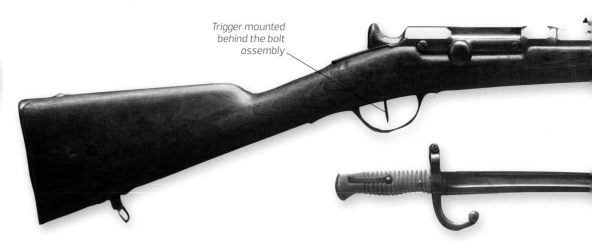

The bolt assembly had a segmented rubber ring that expanded when the gun was fired, sealing the gases inside the barrel and so increasing the velocity of the bullet, but which then shrank to make opening the breech easier

Trigger mounted behind the bolt assembly

Belt loop

LEBEL MODEL 1886

Nearly 3 million examples of the Lebel Model 1886 Rifle were made and nearly all of them entered service with the French Army. The rifle was developed to take advantage of the new smokeless powder, which was three times as powerful as the traditional black powder. It used the then revolutionary copper-jacketed lead bullet that—unlike older lead bullets—would not melt in the barrel when fired at the very high velocities that the new powder made possible. It was, therefore, the most modern rifle in the world. By 1907, however, the Lebel was starting to be outclassed by more modern rifles and the French began developing a successor. The process was not yet complete when war came in 1914, so many Frenchmen marched to war with this rifle.

Flanged barrel to dissipate heat

Pistol grip

Tripod support

COLT-BROWNING M1895

The Colt-Browning M1895 Machine Gun was an American weapon that was used widely by Allied armies during World War I. It was designed by John Browning, and manufactured by Colt. The weapon could fire 400 rounds per minute and was accurate to about 500 yards. The automatic action was unique, being similar to that of the lever-action repeating rifles that Browning had been making for Winchester before he moved to Colt. The result was a fairly slow rate of fire, but one that rarely jammed. The M1895 was used by France at the outbreak of war in 1914 and was at various times also used by Britain, Greece, Russia, Italy, and Uruguay.

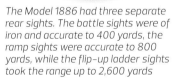

Bayonet, with distinctive downward curve to blade

CHASSEPOT AND BAYONET

When it entered service with the French Army in 1867, the *Chassepot* was the finest rifle in the world. It combined a breech-loading bolt action with a cylindrical bullet that was more accurate in flight than the old balls. The original Chassepot used a paper cartridge, but after 1874 the breech was adapted to use brass cartridges. This new version was officially dubbed the *Gras* Rifle, but it was otherwise identical to the Chassepot. The French retired the Gras from service by 1890 and sold their stocks to Greece, Russia, and Ethiopia, whose armies kept it in service through to World War II.

Wooden stock

The Model 1886 had three separate rear sights. The battle sights were of iron and accurate to 400 yards, the ramp sights were accurate to 800 yards, while the flip-up ladder sights took the range up to 2,600 yards

Bronze handle

LEBEL BAYONET

The introduction to the French Army of the Lebel Model 1886 necessitated a new bayonet. The old-style sword bayonet was discarded and a spike bayonet adopted instead. The early models had a blade just over 20 inches in length with a cruciform cross section and a bronze handle. The experience of trench warfare showed this to be too long to be wielded easily, so the length was reduced to 15 inches. The weapon was widely nicknamed the Rosalie, after the patron saint of the town of Bayonne where some versions were made.

THE BATTLE OF VERDUN

For the French Army, the climax of World War I came at Verdun in 1916. Verdun was a fortified town: it was surrounded by massive fortifications that commanded the River Meuse and had featured in many previous campaigns. The German commander in chief, Erich von Falkenheyn, calculated that the French would never willingly surrender Verdun. He therefore decided to attack the town, though with no intention of capturing it. Instead he wanted to lure the French into sending vast numbers of reserves into the cramped salient in the front lines, where they could be massacred by heavy German guns with little cost to the German Army. The campaign began in February 1916 and French casualties were indeed so heavy that many regiments mutinied and the French Army came close to collapse. In July, the British Army launched the Battle of the Somme and the Germans were forced to move artillery and reserves away from Verdun. As a consequence the battle began to die down and the French Army did not collapse. Falkenheyn called off the campaign in December having inflicted more than half-a-million casualties on the French.

Germany

The German Army, the *Heer*, began both World War I and World War II with sweeping advances and victories that amazed the world, yet it eventually lost both wars. In each instance the initial victories were due to a combination of high-quality training, first-class equipment, and novel tactics, while in both wars the ultimate defeat was due to Germany lacking the resources to endure a long, costly war. In general, it was German use of new weaponry—notably aircraft and tanks—that gave them an advantage over their opponents in 1939–1942, but the excellence of their infantry sidearms was also a significant factor.

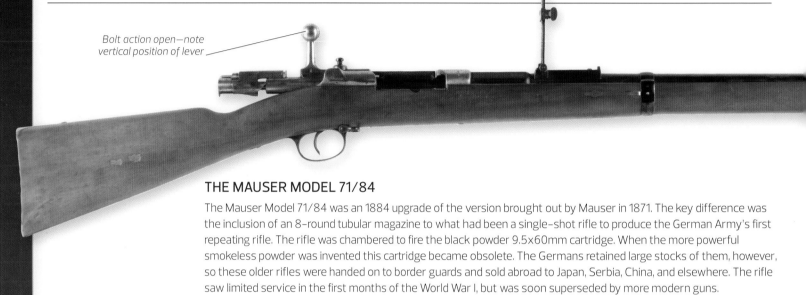

Bolt action open—note vertical position of lever

THE MAUSER MODEL 71/84

The Mauser Model 71/84 was an 1884 upgrade of the version brought out by Mauser in 1871. The key difference was the inclusion of an 8-round tubular magazine to what had been a single-shot rifle to produce the German Army's first repeating rifle. The rifle was chambered to fire the black powder 9.5x60mm cartridge. When the more powerful smokeless powder was invented this cartridge became obsolete. The Germans retained large stocks of them, however, so these older rifles were handed on to border guards and sold abroad to Japan, Serbia, China, and elsewhere. The rifle saw limited service in the first months of the World War I, but was soon superseded by more modern guns.

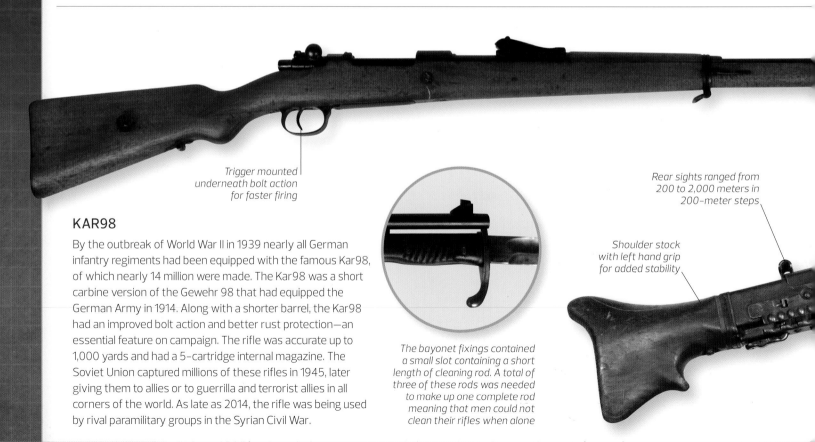

Trigger mounted underneath bolt action for faster firing

Rear sights ranged from 200 to 2,000 meters in 200-meter steps

Shoulder stock with left hand grip for added stability

KAR98

By the outbreak of World War II in 1939 nearly all German infantry regiments had been equipped with the famous Kar98, of which nearly 14 million were made. The Kar98 was a short carbine version of the Gewehr 98 that had equipped the German Army in 1914. Along with a shorter barrel, the Kar98 had an improved bolt action and better rust protection—an essential feature on campaign. The rifle was accurate up to 1,000 yards and had a 5-cartridge internal magazine. The Soviet Union captured millions of these rifles in 1945, later giving them to allies or to guerrilla and terrorist allies in all corners of the world. As late as 2014, the rifle was being used by rival paramilitary groups in the Syrian Civil War.

The bayonet fixings contained a small slot containing a short length of cleaning rod. A total of three of these rods was needed to make up one complete rod meaning that men could not clean their rifles when alone

Attachment point for optional telescopic sights

Optional rifle stock replaces twin hand grips

Water jacket around the barrel holds about one gallon of water

Slot for belt feed

The Mauser 71/84 was the first model to feature the wing safety lever behind the bolt that was to become a standard feature on later Mausers

SPANDAU MAXIM

The MG08 Spandau was the main German machine gun of World War I. It was developed in 1908 from the original 1884 Maxim gun, and so is sometimes called the Spandau Maxim. The gun could fire 500 rounds per minute from a 500-round canvas belt. It was accurate to an imposing 2,000 yards and had a maximum range of 4,000 yards, making this perhaps the most effective machine gun of World War I. It was, however, heavy and required four men to carry it around. This gun was used mostly in static defenses, where it proved to be preeminent. It remained in service with the German Army to 1945, by which date some 170,000 had been made.

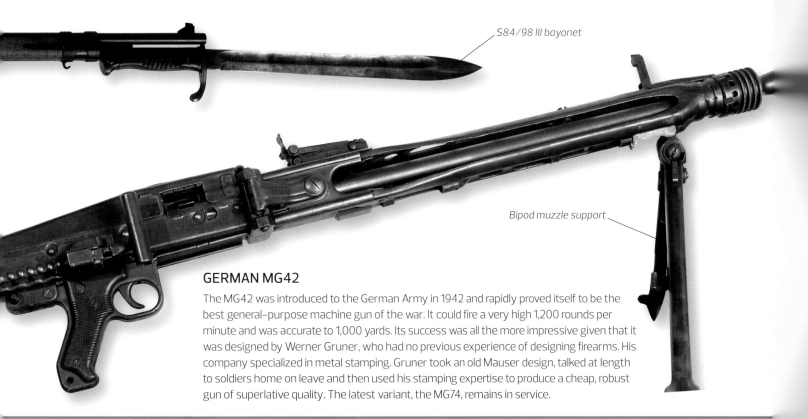

S84/98 III bayonet

Bipod muzzle support

GERMAN MG42

The MG42 was introduced to the German Army in 1942 and rapidly proved itself to be the best general-purpose machine gun of the war. It could fire a very high 1,200 rounds per minute and was accurate to 1,000 yards. Its success was all the more impressive given that it was designed by Werner Gruner, who had no previous experience of designing firearms. His company specialized in metal stamping. Gruner took an old Mauser design, talked at length to soldiers home on leave and then used his stamping expertise to produce a cheap, robust gun of superlative quality. The latest variant, the MG74, remains in service.

The First Submachine Gun

The MP18 was the world's first submachine gun. It entered service with the German Army in 1918 specifically to be used by stormtroopers employing their new and highly effective assault tactics. It could fire 500 rounds per minute, using a 32-cartridge detachable drum magazine that could be quickly and easily replaced by another to maintain the rate of fire. The reliability, fire rate and lightness of this machine gun became legendary and spurred a rush among other countries to produce a comparable machine gun firing pistol-grade ammunition; the British simply copied the MP18. Variants of the MP18 remained in service with the German Army through to 1945.

Brass capped wooden stock

Traditional wooden rifle-style body

STORMTROOPER TACTICS 1917

The failure of massed-infantry assaults on the trenches of the Western Front in 1916 convinced the German high command that any such attacks were doomed to be costly failures. They turned to a concept developed in 1915 by Major Calsow and Captain Rohr, which had earlier been ignored. The new tactics were soon dubbed "stormtrooper." They called for an assault to be led by men equipped with numerous hand grenades and mortars as well as with short carbines and bayonets or submachine guns. These men would push forward, avoiding any strongpoints and instead flowing around any resistance to cut off and surround the enemy. The units were encouraged to blur the distinction between officer and men, boosting initiative and innovation. The stormtroopers achieved some success in 1917, but were most effective in the great Operation Michael of March 1918 when they smashed straight through the British lines. The offensive failed, however, when reinforcements could not be brought up fast enough.

BERGMANN MP18
The Bergmann MP18 was developed by Louis Schmeisser in 1917 as a compact yet highly effective weapon for short-range fighting in trench warfare.

MAGAZINE
The detachable drum magazine was easily replaced and so helped maintain a rate of fire of 500 rounds per minute. Post-war versions used a side-mounted box magazine.

Perforated barrel sleeve allows free movement of air

LUGER PISTOL
The drum magazine used on the MP18 Submachine Gun was originally designed for Luger's Parabellum pistol. Both guns fired the standard pistol cartridges.

PERFORATED BARREL
A shoulder-sling loop is attached beneath the barrel. The barrel jacket is perforated to avoid overheating.

Steel tip

Decorative tassel

MAUSER BAYONET

In 1898 the German Army speculated that its most-likely serious opponent was going to be France. Infantry tacticians believed that the overall length of a rifle and bayonet needed to be the same length as that of an average French soldier. Since the German rifle was some inches shorter than the French, the bayonet had to be correspondingly longer. In 1914, it was very quickly realized that the M1898 bayonet was so slender that it was prone to bend or break on campaign. By 1915, it had been replaced by the shorter model shown here. The sawtooth back was intended to be used to saw up wood, either for firewood or to make posts for barbed wire entanglements.

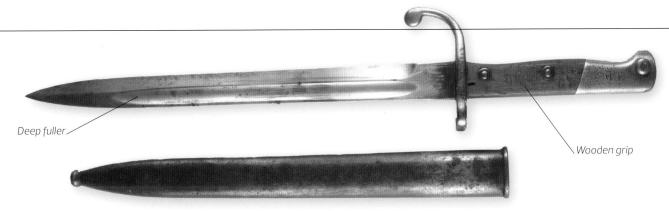

Deep fuller

Wooden grip

BAYONET AND SHEATH

An example of the Weyersberg Kirschbaum & Co Solingen bayonet with sheath. This bayonet was produced in 1891 and was designed for use with the Mauser rifles. Tens of thousands of these bayonets were produced, each stamped with its individual code number on the blade. It was recognized as a robust and effective weapon that could be used as a fighting or general-purpose knife as well as a bayonet. By 1914, the main German Army had replaced these bayonets and the rifles they served, though large numbers saw action in the colonial conflicts of World War I.

Steel blade

Iron sheath

BAYONET AND SHEATH

Produced to be used with the Kar98, the standard German rifle of World War II, this bayonet was made in France during the German occupation. It has a 10 inch blade with a flat back that tapers to a double-edged point. During the Occupation, and particularly after the middle of 1942, the Germans made ruthless use of French factories and workers to help their own war effort. Raw materials were poured into making weapons such as this, while factories producing more peaceful products were closed down or starved of materials.

Plastic barrel rest

Metal stock in folded position

Fore sight

Rear sight

Box magazine holding 32 rounds

MP40

The MP40 was developed for the use of German paratroops and officers in World War II. It was a simplified version of the MP38, and most of the changes were designed to make it cheaper to produce. It could fire 500 rounds per minute, had a 32-round magazine and was accurate to around 100 yards. Later in the war, experience of urban fighting showed that the MP40 was better in such conditions than the standard infantry rifle, so in specialist assault units the automatic weapons were given to every member, not just officers. A major weakness of the design was that the magazine was in a handy position for a handle, but if used in this way it would shake loose and come away. Although this gun is widely called a Schmeisser, the talented gun designer Hugo Schmeisser did not design it.

BLITZKRIEG

At the outbreak of World War II Germany's strategy was to defeat its enemies in a series of Blitzkrieg, "lightning war", strikes that concentrated rapid aircraft, tank, and artillery fire along a narrow front. The intention was to drive a breach in enemy defenses, allowing armored tank divisions to wreak havoc behind enemy lines., causing shock and disorganization and destroying enemy morale. Germany successfully deployed this tactic against Poland, Denmark, Norway, Belgium, the Netherlands, Luxembourg, France, Yugoslavia, and Greece in campaigns from 1939 to 1941. At first, the Blitzkrieg seemed to succeed against Russia when Soviet forces were initially driven back more than 600 miles to the gates of Moscow.

Italy

The Italian armed forces came out of both World Wars with a poor reputation for fighting efficiency. The problem was not so much the poor quality of the training given to the men, which was often of a high standard. Nor were the Italian weapons themselves either poorly designed or obsolete. Rather, the main problem was the bad quality of the manufacturing of the weapons. Some of the blame for this can be attributed to the fact that Italy industrialized fairly

late for a European country, so manufacturing techniques and engineering quality control were not as advanced as they were in Germany, Britain, or France. The men themselves often blamed corruption in the government for the fact that they were sent into battle with weapons that broke or jammed with alarming frequency. It was therefore understandable that the Italians often preferred to surrender rather than risk their lives on the reliability of their weapons.

MANNLICHER-CARCANO

The Mannlicher-Carcano rifle was developed in 1891 to fire the 6.5x52mm copper-jacketed cartridge that used the then new smokeless powder. It was a development of the Austrian Mannlicher rifle made by Salvatore Carcano at the official Italian Arsenal in Turin. In effect, therefore, it was derived from the German Mauser design. It was accurate to about 700 yards and had a 6-round internal magazine. By 1938 the Mannlicher-Carcano was considered to be rather old fashioned, so the Italian Army began designing a replacement. That was not ready when World War II began, so the Italians went to war in 1940 with the same rifle as they did in 1915. Production ceased in 1945 but some of these guns are still used by paramilitaries in North Africa.

Spur on trigger guard to be gripped by fingers for added stability

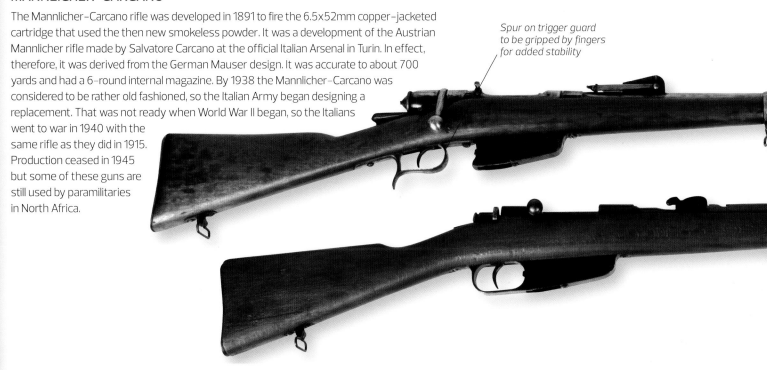

Muzzle brake

GERMAN SOLOTHURN S18-1000

The Solothurn S18-1000 was developed in Switzerland by Solothurn, a wholly owned subsidiary of the German Rheinmetall company. Anti-tank weapons were not permitted to be made in Germany under the terms of the Versailles Treaty, which ended World War I, hence the Swiss base for the weapon. It was bought in numbers by the Italians and Finns. The weapon fired a 20mm projectile with a self-loading repeating action from a 10-round magazine. It was claimed that it could penetrate 20mm of armor at 100 yards, which made it effective against many pre-war tank designs, but by 1941 new types of tank had thicker armor and this weapon was withdrawn from service.

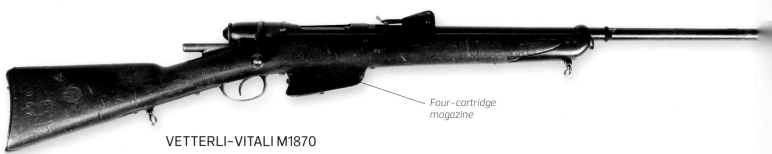

Four-cartridge magazine

VETTERLI-VITALI M1870

In 1870, the newly united Kingdom of Italy needed a modern rifle for its army. The one chosen was the Vetterli-Vitali M1870, a variant of the Swiss Vetterli M69, which was the world's first repeating rifle to have a self-cocking action enabling a man to fire rapidly and accurately. The Vitali's simplified design was capable of being manufactured cheaply and reliably by Italian factories which were not of the same standard as those in Switzerland. It was at first a single-shot rifle, but in 1887 a four-cartridge magazine was added to produce the M1870/87 shown here. This rifle was retired from service when the Mannlicher-Carcano became available. However, when Italy joined World War I in 1915 large numbers of reservists were called up and equipped with the M1870/87.

Cleaning rod

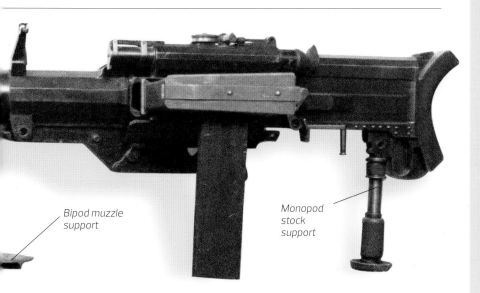

Bipod muzzle support

Monopod stock support

BATTLE OF VITTORIO VENETO

In June 1918 the Austro-Hungarian Army in northern Italy launched a major offensive designed to knock Italy out of the war. The assault failed with heavy losses, and the Italians began planning a massive counterattack. They chose to attack across the Piave River at Vittorio Veneto, aiming to exploit the junction between two Austro-Hungarian sectors. The Italian attack began on October 24 with a diversion on Monte Grappa, which attracted Austrian reserves. The main assault was then unleashed three days later. As the Italians advanced, politics came into play. On October 28 Czechoslovakia declared itself independent of the Austro-Hungarian Empire, followed next day by Yugoslavia and then by Hungary. The Austro-Hungarian Army then collapsed as vast numbers of men simply started walking home. An armistice was agreed on November 3, but by then the war was already effectively over.

Japan

Japan joined World War I as an ally of Britain, but played little part in any serious fighting. The Japanese Navy seized German island colonies in the Pacific, but Japan's main occupation was increasing her diplomatic and business interests in Asia while the European powers were busy fighting. In 1937, Japan took advantage of chaos in China to invade northern provinces of that country, thereby starting a war with China that would drag on for years. In 1941, Japan took the fateful step of attacking the USA and Britain with the aim of achieving a vast sphere of influence and creating an empire in the western Pacific. The fighting that followed took place from the chilly Aleutian Islands to the hot, humid jungles of New Guinea.

JAPANESE PARATROOP RIFLE

During the 1930s, several countries experimented with transporting infantry by air, landing them in combat zones either by glider or parachute. Finding equipment that was small and light enough to carry on aircraft was a common problem. The Japanese solved the issue with the Arisaka Type 2 Paratroop Rifle. The gun comes apart just behind the barrel, so that the rear half contains the bolt mechanism, trigger assembly, and butt while the front has the barrel and stock. The two halves were held together by a screw–in metal wedge.

Gun comes apart just behind the barrel

The rear sights of the Type 38 were standard ladder sights. They could be removed and replaced with telescopic sights of a model first used in 1938. The factory conversions with telescopic sights were designated the Type 97, though they were otherwise identical to the Type 38

Bolt mechanism in closed position

BATTLE OF THE SITTANG BRIDGE

In January 1942 Japanese troops based in Thailand invaded Burma, which was then a British colony. The Japanese advanced rapidly, driving the British-Indian 17th Division toward the wide and unfordable Sittang River. There was only one bridge over the river, and on the morning of February 22 the Japanese launched a determined attack to capture it. Fearing the bridge would fall into Japanese hands the British officer on the spot blew it up, stranding most of the 17th Division on the wrong side of the river. The Japanese victory was widely held to be due to the fact that their small arms and training made them better at jungle fighting than the British-Indian forces they faced.

25-inch barrel with front sight protected by metal "ears"

Release catch to allow gun to be separated into two sections

Cleaning rod

Barrel of carbine version is shorter than standard

JAPANESE TYPE 38

The Type 38 was the standard rifle of the Japanese infantry from 1905 to 1945. The rifle was over 50 inches long, making this the longest rifle used in World War II, and carried a 15-inch bayonet. It fired the relatively weak Ariska 6.5x50mm cartridge, giving it a limited range. Japanese training put an emphasis on close-quarter combat, so a long-range rifle was not considered necessary, though a long reach for the bayonet was. A carbine variant more than 12 inches shorter was produced for use by cavalry, artillery gunners, and engineers.

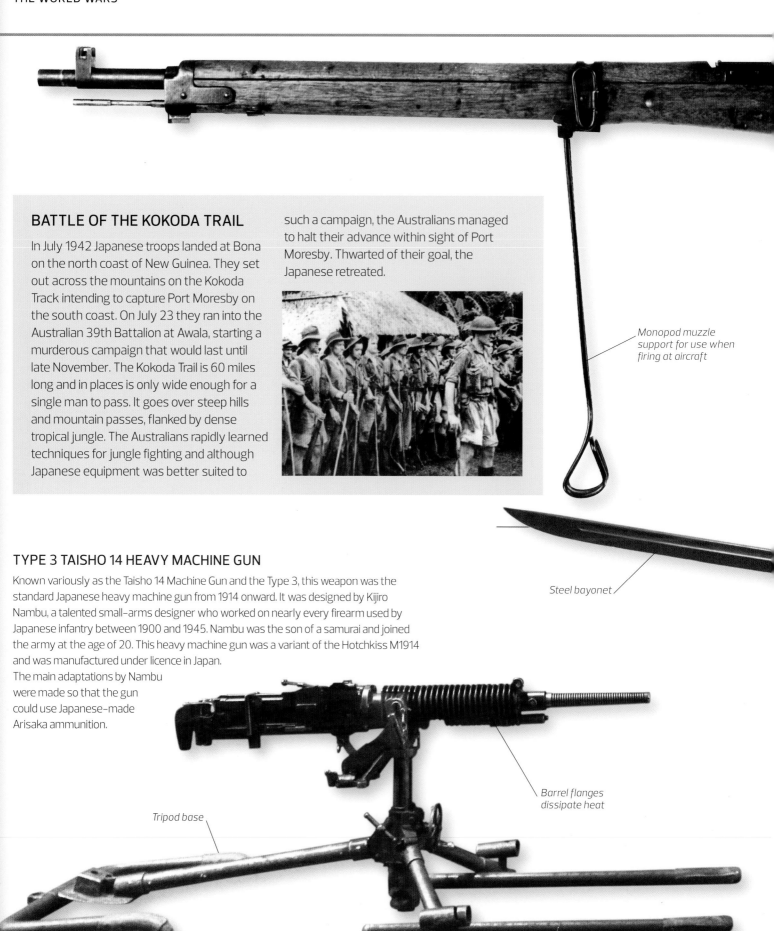

BATTLE OF THE KOKODA TRAIL

In July 1942 Japanese troops landed at Bona on the north coast of New Guinea. They set out across the mountains on the Kokoda Track intending to capture Port Moresby on the south coast. On July 23 they ran into the Australian 39th Battalion at Awala, starting a murderous campaign that would last until late November. The Kokoda Trail is 60 miles long and in places is only wide enough for a single man to pass. It goes over steep hills and mountain passes, flanked by dense tropical jungle. The Australians rapidly learned techniques for jungle fighting and although Japanese equipment was better suited to such a campaign, the Australians managed to halt their advance within sight of Port Moresby. Thwarted of their goal, the Japanese retreated.

Monopod muzzle support for use when firing at aircraft

Steel bayonet

TYPE 3 TAISHO 14 HEAVY MACHINE GUN

Known variously as the Taisho 14 Machine Gun and the Type 3, this weapon was the standard Japanese heavy machine gun from 1914 onward. It was designed by Kijiro Nambu, a talented small-arms designer who worked on nearly every firearm used by Japanese infantry between 1900 and 1945. Nambu was the son of a samurai and joined the army at the age of 20. This heavy machine gun was a variant of the Hotchkiss M1914 and was manufactured under licence in Japan. The main adaptations by Nambu were made so that the gun could use Japanese-made Arisaka ammunition.

Barrel flanges dissipate heat

Tripod base

Disk-shaped safety catch at rear of bolt

Close up of bolt handle in closed position

JAPANESE TYPE 99

The Type 99 rifle was introduced to the Japanese Army in 1939. It was originally intended that it should replace the Type 38 by 1943, but the outbreak of war against the USA and Britain in 1941 forced the Japanese to keep both rifles in service. The Type 99 was a robust weapon that was well able to cope with the difficult jungle and tropical conditions in which it was so often used. The barrel of early models had a chrome lining to help with cleaning and to prolong the life of the weapon. By 1943, shortages resulting from the American submarine warfare on Japanese merchant shipping meant that the chrome lining had to be abandoned.

Carrying handle

Flip-up rear sight

Folding bipod muzzle support

Barrel with integrated cooling flanges to dissipate the heat generated by rapid fire

Wooden hand grip

TYPE 96 LIGHT MACHINE GUN

By 1935 the Japanese Type 11 light machine gun had been recognized as being too prone to jamming to be a reliable weapon of war. The Type 96 entered production in 1936 as a replacement. Its role was to provide close support to infantry formations, and was carried rapidly into action by a two-man crew. It was based on the French Hotchkiss M1909, but with certain alterations to suit Japanese-produced ammunition. The gun came with several barrels, which could be swapped over quickly when one grew warm and threatened to jam due to overheating. The gun proved to be popular with troops since it was rugged and reliable, though it had a fairly limited range compared to the American weapons it faced.

Russia

In both world wars the Russians entered the war with poorly trained men, obsolete equipment and, among their generals, widespread incompetence. These deficiencies led to some catastrophic early defeats, which saw their opponents drive deep into Russia, capturing vast numbers of prisoners and valuable natural resources on the way. In both wars it was the vast open spaces that saved Russia, allowing their armies to fall back without being overwhelmed. During World War I, the Russian state collapsed into civil war in 1917 and surrendered, while in World War II it remained united and fought through to ultimate victory. The rifles and other infantry weapons used by the Russian armies in both wars were of reasonably good quality, it was in heavy weaponry that the main weaknesses existed.

Rear ladder sights graduated from 100 to 2,000 meters

The bolt handle on the Mosin-Nagant is unique in being fixed to a protrusion on the center of the bolt. The bolt can be removed by pulling it fully back and then squeezing the trigger

Hooded post front sight

Magazine holding 5 rounds

MOSIN-NAGANT 1891

Russian infantry, armed with single-shot rifles, suffered heavy casualties when facing Turks with Winchester repeating rifles during the Russo-Turkish War of 1877–78. The subsequent trials to find a new rifle were won by Sergei Mosin with a .30 caliber bolt-action repeating rifle. However, Mosin's design had a magazine that fell apart easily, so the magazine of the losing rifle designed by Belgian Leon Nagant was used instead. The resulting rifle was dubbed the Mosin-Nagant and entered service in 1891. This example is a Model 1891 infantry rifle. The Model 1891 was also produced as a cavalry carbine and a cossack carbine, as well as a very short carbine for the artillery. It was with these firearms that the Tsar's armies marched to war in 1914.

BATTLE OF STALINGRAD

Thwarted in his attempts to capture Moscow in December 1941, Hitler drew up new strategic aims for the war against Russia in 1942. A massive offensive was planned in the south to capture the strategic grainfields and coalmines of the Crimea before crossing the Volga to take the vital Caucasian oil fields and put German troops at the southern end of the Urals, thus poised to destroy the Russians in 1943. It was a good plan, but it hinged on capturing the city of Stalingrad. Realizing this, the Russians threw their maximum effort into defending the city. By November 1942 the German assault on the city had been halted, so the Soviets launched a counter-offensive, which trapped 250,000 Germans in Stalingrad. The street fighting that followed was savage and merciless. Only 6,000 Germans survived. Urban fighting required weapons that were effective at short ranges and were easy to handle in confined spaces, quite unlike the weapons that the Germans had perfected for rapidly moving blitzkrieg tactics.

MOSIN-NAGANT M91/30/59

In 1930, the Mosin-Nagant Model 1891 underwent a redesign to produce the M91/30. The changes were mostly to the sights, which were recalibrated in meters in place of the traditional Russian arshini unit (which measured about 72cm) and the receiver was changed to a round shape instead of the original octagon. Many millions of this model were produced before, during and after World War II as it became the standard rifle of the Red Army. In 1959, about a million of these rifles were sent to Bulgaria where the barrel was shortened and a new foresight fitted. This is an example of one of these Bulgarian adaptations, known as the M91/30/59.

Permanently attached bayonet slides back to lie alongside right side of barrel when not in use

RUSSIAN M1944

The savage street fighting that took place in Stalingrad and other Russian cities during 1942 and 1943 showed that the standard Russian Mosin-Nagant rifle was too long for use in confined spaces like rooms, alleyways, and sewers. The carbine version lacked a bayonet and so was of little use. The need for a better urban weapon led to the M1944 carbine. The weapon was basically a cut down Mosin-Nagant rifle with a 20-inch barrel fitted with a folding bayonet that when folded fitted into a notch on the wooden stock. In 1943, some 50,000 of the M1944 were produced and issued to frontline troops. These were so successful that 3.6 million were made in 1944 and 3.4 million the following year. This fell to 190,000 in the first year of peace.

DEGTYAREV DP MODEL 1928

Introduced in 1928 the DP was a light machine gun that saw extensive service with the Red Army. It was designed to use the 7.62x54mm cartridge that the Red Army was adopting in the 1920s. From the start, simplicity and cheapness of manufacture were key considerations. Despite this the weapon proved to be a reliable one. It could fire 600 rounds per minute over 800 yards, and was relatively impervious to dust and mud.

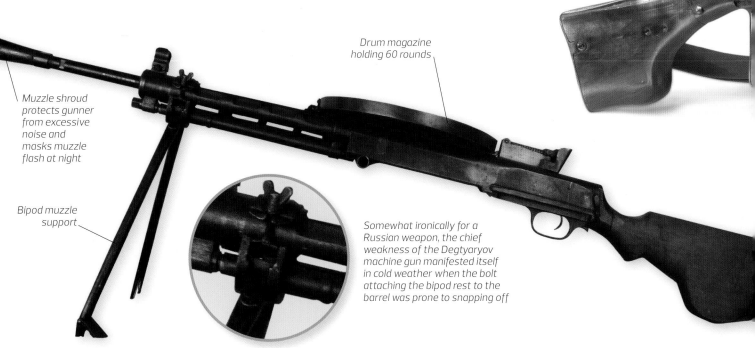

Drum magazine holding 60 rounds

Muzzle shroud protects gunner from excessive noise and masks muzzle flash at night

Bipod muzzle support

Somewhat ironically for a Russian weapon, the chief weakness of the Degtyaryov machine gun manifested itself in cold weather when the bolt attaching the bipod rest to the barrel was prone to snapping off

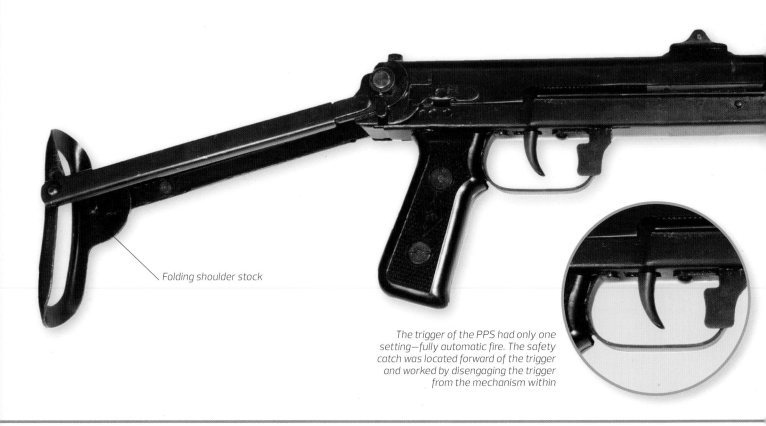

Folding shoulder stock

The trigger of the PPS had only one setting—fully automatic fire. The safety catch was located forward of the trigger and worked by disengaging the trigger from the mechanism within

Bipod muzzle support

The central wooden handle was designed for lifting the machine gun from one position to another, however in combat soldiers often used this as a second hand grip to allow the weapon to be fire from the hip

Drum magazine holding 100 rounds

RPD MACHINE GUN

Entering service just as World War II ended, the RPD light machine gun was developed to replace the DP Model 1928. The initials stand for Ruchnoy Pulemyot Degtyaryova, which translates as "hand-held machine gun of Degtyaryov" and it neatly encapsulates what the gun's designer Vasily Degtyaryov was hoping to achieve. The gun can fire 750 rounds per minute from a 100-round drum magazine and is accurate to up to 1,000 yards. Add to this the fact that it fires the 7.62x54mm cartridge and the weapon comes out as significantly heavier and more accurate than contemporary submachine guns, though it was still light enough to be held by a single man. No longer in service with the Russian Army, it has been passed on to Russian allies.

Muzzle brake reduces recoil

The PPS was intended to be held in two hands when fired. The housing which locked the magazine into position was intended to double as the forward handle

Detachable box magazine with 35 rounds

PPS SUBMACHINE GUN

As the German Army surged deep into Russia in 1941, it became very clear that rear-area personnel were in desperate need of a personal-protection weapon of some kind to use when German troops appeared unexpectedly. The need to have it as soon as possible meant the new gun had to be cheap and easy to make using non-skilled labor, and to fire the 7.62x25mm round that was also cheap and easy to manufacture. The result was the PPS submachine gun. The gun could fire 100 rounds per minute and was accurate to 200 yards. Always a rough and ready weapon, the PPS was taken out of Red Army use when the war ended. The vast numbers produced were then passed on to Soviet allies, seeing service with the Viet Cong, Chinese. and Albanians, among many others.

USA

The United States of America was not involved in the initial stages of either World War. In both 1914 and 1939 many Americans viewed the unfolding conflicts as a purely European affair and did not wish to get involved. The USA joined World War I in 1917 after German submarines began targeting US merchant ships and when it became known that Germany had offered Mexico money and arms to attack the USA. In 1941 it was the Japanese attack on Pearl Harbor that brought America into the fighting. On both occasions the Americans rapidly expanded all branches of their armed forces by means of the massive financial, industrial, and manpower resources at its disposal. Innovations in weapon design and tactics proved to be an American strength, making up for what were initially small numbers of armed forces.

LOST BATTALION OF THE ARGONNE

In October 1918, a battalion of Americans under Major Charles Whittlesey advanced into the Argonne Forest with French units on their flank. The French failed to keep up and the Americans were rapidly surrounded by a German counterattack. At first it was assumed that the unit had surrendered, but then a carrier pigeon got through announcing that they were still fighting—although short of food and water. For six days the Americans held out against repeated attacks until a new American offensive got through to them. No fewer than seven men were awarded the Medal of Honor in this action. Whittlesey put the survival of his men down to the use of the M1918 BAR.

Wooden hand grip

Bipod muzzle support

Detachable magazine

The Eddystone Enfield had the rear sights positioned at the rear of the breech which proved to be much more accurate than the mid-barrel sights of the original Enfield

Bolt action in open position

Breech

Trigger guard

Gas piston under barrel

Removable barrel

The rear arm of the tripod mounting included lugs to which the padded seat for the gunner was fixed

Pistol grip

Tripod support

MARLIN MACHINE GUN

The version of the M1895 Colt–Browning machine gun produced for the US Army was dubbed the "Potato Digger" because of the lever under the barrel that snapped up and down as the weapon was fired. This unusual action made for a light-weight construction and meant that the weapon could fire upward of a thousand rounds without stopping to allow the mechanism to cool. While these were both important advantages, the mechanism did mean that the gun had to be mounted on a tripod that allowed enough space for the lever to work. In turn this meant the men operating the gun sat high off the ground, and so were vulnerable to incoming fire.

Finger grips

Iron ring with attachment for sling

Front sights

EDDYSTONE ENFIELD

Officially the US Rifle Model 1917, this rifle was widely dubbed the Eddystone Enfield since it was a version of the British Lee–Enfield made at the Remington works in Eddystone, Pennsylvania. The only real changes to the British design were to adapt the gun to fire the .30-06 Springfield cartridge widely used by the US Army. The US Army did not care for the British bayonet and so produced the new M1917 bayonet to fit this gun. That bayonet proved to be so versatile that it was later used for a wide range of firearms and remains in service.

Flash suppressor
fitted to muzzle

Barrel lacks
bayonet mounting

Wooden
hand grip

BATTLE OF IWO JIMA

On February 19, 1945 US Marines landed on the Pacific island of Iwo Jima, aiming to capture its three airfields for use in the bombing campaign against Japan. The Japanese defense proved to be tenacious and skilled, with heavy fortifications, hidden gun positions, and fanatical bravery. The US Marines were armed with M1 Garard rifles and BAR machine guns. The campaign took more than a month and cost both sides over 25,000 casualties. One of the most iconic photos of the war was taken by Joe Rosenthal and showed US Marines raising the American flag on the top of Mount Suribachi.

Front post sights

Bipod muzzle support

The flash suppressor was fitted from 1918 onward in an effort to dissipate the flash that emerged from the muzzle and which combat experience had shown tended to dazzle the gun's user in poor light conditions

BROWNING AUTOMATIC WITH SUPPORT

Although it was intended to be carried and used by a single infantryman as he walked, the BAR was soon superseded in that role by submachine guns. Instead it was redesigned to operate as a light machine gun firing from a bipod support, as shown here. It was widely used in this role during World War II as well as in the Korean and Vietnam Wars. Large numbers of this variant were sold to prison services, banks, and private security firms as a weapon to be mounted in permanent guard positions to protect buildings across the USA.

BROWNING AUTOMATIC

When the US Army began preparing to go to Europe in 1917 it was decided that there was a need for a machine gun light enough to be carried by a single soldier as he advanced toward enemy trenches. The result was the M1918 Browning Automatic Rifle, or BAR. Designed by John Browning, the gun could fire 500 rounds per minute from a 20-round detachable magazine to ranges of 1,000 yards. The weight of the gun was around 16 pounds, and it was supplied with a shoulder strap so that it could be carried at the hip, then lifted to the shoulder to be fired. The gun later went through a wide variety of variants, some remaining in use to the 1990s.

Folding rear sights

Butt plate is hinged to help stabilize the weapon against the marksman's shoulder

Detachable magazine holding 20 rounds

Muzzle guard

Barrel flanges
dissipate heat

Forward hand grip
for better aim

Box magazine

AUDIE MURPHY

Audie Murphy was the most decorated combat
soldier of World War II, earning most of his medals
while armed with an M1 Garard rifle, and some with
a Tommy gun. Murphy entered combat in Sicily in
1943, later fighting in Italy, southern France, and
Germany. Writing later of combat, Murphy said "I
remember the experience as I do a nightmare. A
demon seems to have entered my body. My brain is
coldly alert and logical. I do not think of the danger to
myself. My whole being is concentrated on killing."
After the war he enjoyed a successful acting career
in Hollywood, usually in war or cowboy movies.

Safety catch
at front of
trigger guard

Hand guard

Wooden stock

The Tommy Gun is most familiar in gangster movies with the optional drum magazine which held 100 rounds it was found in military use that a half-empty magazine produced a rattling noise that was too loud for clandestine operations, so the silent 30 round box magazine was favored instead

THOMPSON

The famous Tommy Gun was officially the Thompson Submachine Gun, though its inventor, General John Thompson, dubbed it "The Annihilator." Thompson wanted a short, light machine gun that could be carried easily in trenches but that had a high rate of fire to spray bullets along a trench to clear it of enemy soldiers. Design work began in 1916, but the war ended before the gun entered production. It was bought by police forces and the US Marines, but its great fame came from the relatively few that were used by gangsters during the Prohibition Era. The British Army bought the weapon in the 1930s, followed by the US Army. This example is an M1928 version with a box magazine, not the more familiar drum magazine.

Front sight

Deep fullered steel bayonet

The M1 was loaded using 8 cartridge clips that was pushed down through the breech and ejected when empty. The ejection of an empty clip produced a distinctive "ping", which alerted enemy soldiers to the fact that the American soldier had an empty gun

M1 GARAND

The M1 Garand was the most common type of US Army rifle in World War II. It entered service in 1936 and remained in use for 40 years. It was a semiautomatic weapon, so the user did not have to operate a bolt between firing, but could simply pull the trigger again. The magazine held eight rounds and was automatically ejected when empty ready for the next to be inserted. This gave the US infantry an advantage over both German and Japanese foes, whose rifles were bolt operated. The gun was accurate to 500 yards, though its maximum range was more than double this distance.

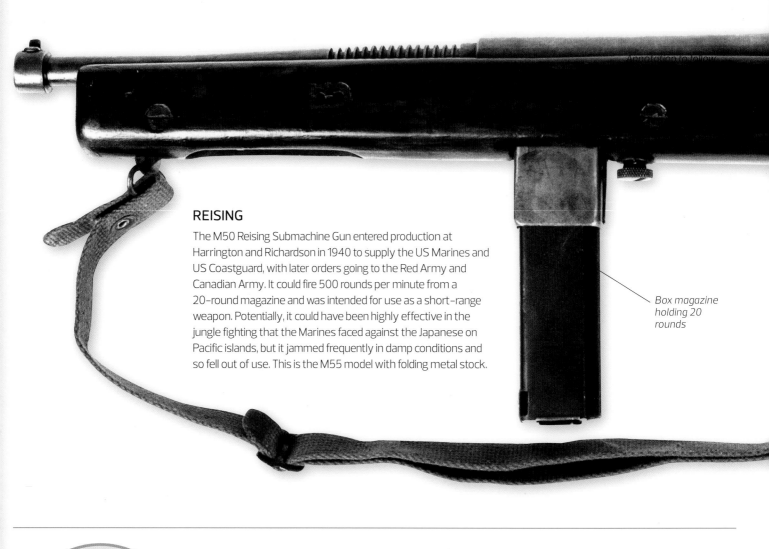

REISING

The M50 Reising Submachine Gun entered production at
Harrington and Richardson in 1940 to supply the US Marines and
US Coastguard, with later orders going to the Red Army and
Canadian Army. It could fire 500 rounds per minute from a
20-round magazine and was intended for use as a short-range
weapon. Potentially, it could have been highly effective in the
jungle fighting that the Marines faced against the Japanese on
Pacific islands, but it jammed frequently in damp conditions and
so fell out of use. This is the M55 model with folding metal stock.

*Box magazine
holding 20
rounds*

LEE-ENFIELD M1917 MKIII

The M1917 was a version of the standard British Lee-Enfield rifle that was
manufactured in the USA from 1917. The model differed from the British-
made original in having a clawed cartridge extractor and rear sights placed
at the back of the rifle instead of in front of the bolt mechanism.

Bolt action

*Integral magazine filled
from 5-round clip*

Folding shoulder stock

Pistol grip

JOHNSON BAYONET

The M1941 Johnson Bayonet was designed specifically for use with the M1941 Johnson Rifle. This weapon was a shorter semiautomatic rifle that lost the competition to supply the US Army to the M1 Garand. It was subsequently sold in small numbers to the Netherlands, Argentina, and other countries. The bayonet has no handle or grip, only a metal tang that fits on to the rifle muzzle. As a consequence it cannot be used by the soldier for any other purpose.

Leather sheath

Bayonet attachment

Model 1917 bayonet

Other Countries

As their names suggest, the two World Wars were global conflicts that involved not just the main combatant states, but also dozens of other countries. Some were involved only in peripheral areas or in specific duties—such as escorting merchant ships at sea—but a surprisingly large number of smaller countries were involved in land warfare and therefore had the need for firearms.

Magazine holds 5 rounds

Barrel 739mm long

Early style fore sight dates this rifle to before 1938

The Swedish Mauser remained in service from 1895 to 1995 in various models. All models retained the original Mauser bolt layout that required the user to lift the bolt handle to the vertical position before the bolt could be slid back to reload the weapon.

40-round magazine

Barrel shroud

Barrel 584mm long

Bipod barrel support

SWEDEN

Sweden remained neutral throughout World War II. The country was surrounded by Axis forces and there was a genuine fear that invasion might come at any time. The Swedish Army manned defensive positions around cities, ports and airports armed with their own Mausers. The Swedish Army was equipped with the Mauser M1894, adapted to fire the 6.5x55mm cartridge that was manufactured locally. Until the end of World War I, these guns were made in Germany, but production then shifted to Sweden where they were made by the Bofors company. By 1939 Bofors were producing short carbine and specialist sniper variants as well as the standard infantry rifle.

THAILAND

In June 1940 Japan occupied the east Asian colonies of France, recently defeated by Germany. Thailand allied itself with Japan and took back provinces lost to France some decades earlier. Japan insisted on stationing troops in Thailand by way of reciprocation. Thailand was never officially at war with the Allies, but was seen as a Japanese ally and there were some clashes. The Thai Army used large numbers of the Madsen Light Machine Gun, a weapon developed in Denmark in 1902 but subsequently sold to many countries. It could fire 400 rounds per minute from a 40-round magazine and was accurate to about 600 yards.

Magazine holds 5 rounds

Rear sights

Barrel 765mm long

BULGARIA

Bulgaria fought on the German side in World War I, but sought to remain neutral in World War II. However, the Bulgarians did send units to occupy Macedonia when Yugoslavia was defeated, and they later allowed German troops to move across their territory. In September 1944 the Russian Army reached Bulgaria. The German Army moved to seize key points in Bulgaria, so Bulgaria declared war on Germany and asked for Russian help. Instead Stalin declared war on Bulgaria and invaded. A Communist government was installed in Bulgaria, which then became a puppet state controlled by the Soviets. Through all this the Bulgarian Army fought with the Mannlicher M95. This rifle was derived from the Steyr–Mannlicher M1895 with which the Austro-Hungarian Empire fought World War I. By 1944, most Bulgarian troops had the shorter carbine version that entered service in 1930 and was known as the M95/30.

Barrel shroud

Barrel length 213mm

Magazine holds up to 40 rounds

ALBANIA

For Albania, World War II began before the rest of Europe became involved. In April 1939, Italy invaded Albania to oust the corrupt King Zog. The war was over in less than a week, but Zog's supporters took to the mountains to fight a guerrilla war. By 1943 Communist guerrillas backed by Russia were also active fighting both the Italians and Zogists. The Germans sent in troops to back the Italians, and then when Italy changed sides, to fight against them. In the autumn of 1944, the Red Army arrived and ruthlessly crushed all resistance to a Communist takeover. The Beretta M38 was an Italian submachine gun sold to the Albanians when the two countries were allies, and which therefore saw action on both sides during the Italian invasion. It was later found in the hands of Communist guerrillas.

Lang Visier rear sights

Magazine holds 5 rounds

Open front sights

Bayonet fixing point

PERSIA

In 1941, the Persian Government sought to take advantage of Britain's weakness by nationalizing the British-owned oil industry. Britain relied on Iranian oil to keep its warships at sea, so despite pressures elsewhere, Britain invaded Persia in August. The war lasted only a few weeks, and through this fighting the Persian infantry used Mausers. These rifles were acquired during the early 1930s and were slightly modernized versions of the Mauser 1898. They were all manufactured in the Czech city of Brno until the German invasion of Czechoslovakia in 1939, after which copies were made in Iran itself.

The Mauser action required the bolt handle to be in a horizontal position to lock the two lugs into place and secure the breech before the weapon could be fired.

Specialist Rifles

The modern rifle developed out of the early 19th-century musket. The key developments in the course of the 19th century were the cheap and reliable rifled barrels combined with breech-loading mechanisms to take the new metal-jacketed cartridges. It was these developments that led to the reliable long-range rifles such as the Mauser and Lee-Enfield that dominated the infantry equipment of the two World Wars. Subsequent improvements have been mostly related to automatic or semiautomatic firing. However, there have also been significant efforts to expand the rifle concept into more specialist fields, often the resulting in personal firearms that have had little relation to the standard rifle.

BREDA M35PG

The Breda M35 PG rifle was a groundbreaking Italian design that never made it into full scale production—only 300 were built—but it was the world's first true selector automatic weapon. Breda was famed for innovative designs, particularly of automatic weapons. This one grew out of a desire for a rifle that could fire single shots and automatic bursts. It had a switch that enabled the gun to fire one round, four successive rounds or to empty the magazine.

Gun fired single solid bullet

Cocking handle

Open-sided magazine caused problems with dirt ingress

Overall length 39 inches

Folding fore sight

Shoulder stock

Monopod support

PIAT

The PIAT was a hand-held British anti-tank weapon. The barrel housed a powerful spring, which pushed a projectile forward and simultaneously set off propellant to power it through the air. When a target was hit, the hollow charge detonated, focusing explosive energy on to the armor and causing a shower of sharp splinters to fly off the inside of the armor to kill the crew. Although effective, its range at 100 yards was short, and by 1944, the Germans had fitted spacer armor to their tanks, which caused projectiles to burst early.

BOYS ANTI-TANK RIFLE

The Boys Anti-Tank Rifle entered service with the British Army in 1937. At that date most armies fielded large numbers of lightly armored tanks and armored cars designed to move fast from one area to another, lending firepower to infantry assaults, or ranging far behind enemy lines to disrupt supply lines. The Boys, firing a solid bullet that could penetrate 20mm of armor at 100 yards, was effective against such vehicles. By 1942, however, these thinner-skinned armored vehicles had been largely abandoned and the Boys was no longer effective against the new heavier tanks. The version shown here is the MkI with a single stick support.

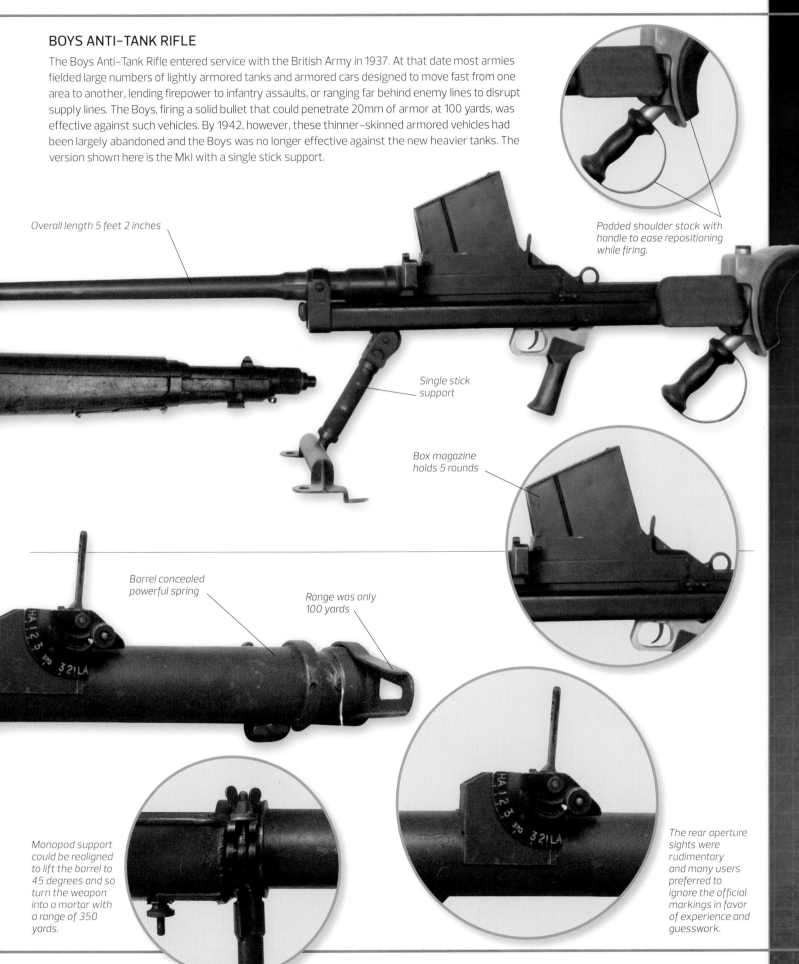

Padded shoulder stock with handle to ease repositioning while firing.

Overall length 5 feet 2 inches

Single stick support

Box magazine holds 5 rounds

Barrel concealed powerful spring

Range was only 100 yards

Monopod support could be realigned to lift the barrel to 45 degrees and so turn the weapon into a mortar with a range of 350 yards.

The rear aperture sights were rudimentary and many users preferred to ignore the official markings in favor of experience and guesswork.

125

PHILIPPINE HUCK GUN

The search for weapons that were cheap to make and needed the minimum of skilled labor in the manufacturing process reached a peak with the Philippine Huck Gun, which has almost no working parts. The barrel comes out of the sleeve, attached to the stock. A bullet is put into the end of the barrel, which is then slid back into the sleeve. When the hand grip on the barrel is jerked backward the base of the cartridge hits a firing pin and the weapon fires. Crude, but effective at close ranges, the Huck gun was widely used by guerrillas resisting the Japanese occupation.

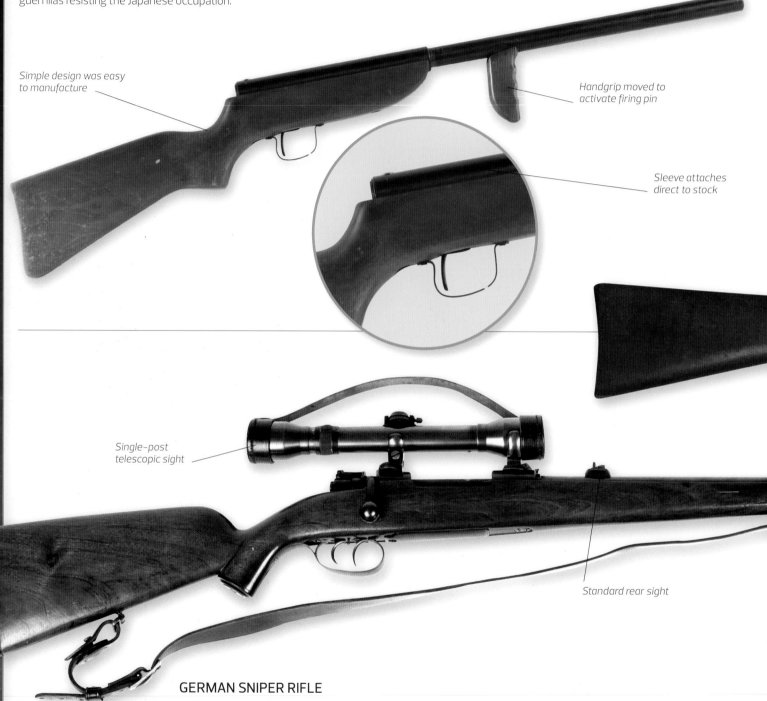

Simple design was easy to manufacture

Handgrip moved to activate firing pin

Sleeve attaches direct to stock

Single-post telescopic sight

Standard rear sight

GERMAN SNIPER RIFLE

During World War II the German Army adapted pre-war Mauser rifles, made originally as civilian hunting and target weapons, for use by snipers. The 8mm Mauser shown here is fitted with a Hensolt single-post telescopic sight. An American officer took this particular rifle from a dead German snipe during the Battle of the Bulge in the winter of 1944-45. The ammunition this rifle, and other German sniper guns, fired was the 7.92x57mm Mauser cartridge developed in 1905. This cartridge was one of the first to have a pointed bullet which, together with the powerful charge of smokeless powder the cartridge contained, resulted in a high velocity bullet with good aerodynamic performance. This made it ideal for sniper use and the cartridge remains in service as a hunting cartridge.

ITALIAN BERETTA M38A SUBMACHINE GUN

The Italian Beretta M38 was perhaps the most successful small arm produced in Italy during World War II. The original pre-war M38 was a fine weapon, but it needed hours of skilled labor to produce, and once Italy joined the war in 1940, such lavish time and cost was no longer affordable. Thus early models, such as this M38A, became highly prized. The later M38/42 lacked a cooling jacket or bayonet fixing point and the internal mechanism was simplified. The M38/43 lacked cooling fins on the barrel and the M38/44 had a simplified recoil system. While each change made the weapon cheaper to produce, each also reduced its effectiveness, with jamming due to overheating being a real problem in later models.

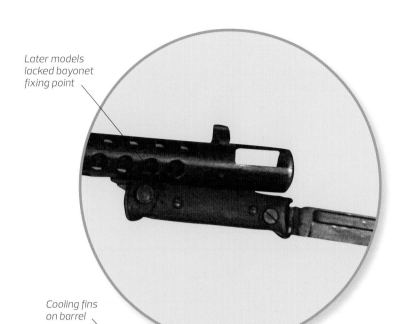

Later models lacked bayonet fixing point

Cooling fins on barrel

Twin triggers, one for single-shot the other for continuous fire.

Built up fore sight

The standard German sniper telescopic sight was the ZF-41. However its poor performance in low-light conditions meant that many German snipers preferred to use sights captured from the Soviets.

RETREAT TO DUNKIRK

In May 1940 the German blitzkrieg cut through the French army on the Meuse, allowing the panzers to head west at high speed to reach the English Channel at Abbeville. The German breakthrough cut off the British and Belgian Armies, and some French units. The British began a fighting retreat to Dunkirk, which was the only port left open to them, so that the Royal Navy could take them home. Slowing down the advance of the panzers was a key aim, and the Boys Anti-Tank Rifle (see page 125) was deployed. The Boys proved to be effective against the Panzer MkII—a light scout tank—but was useless against the more heavily armored MkIII and MkIV. Fortunately for the Allies, German commanders feared that the heavier tanks might become bogged down in the marshy soil around Dunkirk and ordered a halt to panzer attacks, which enabled more troops to be evacuated safely.

Assault Rifles

Early Assault Rifles

Every major army in the world has an assault rifle as the primary arm of its infantry rank and file. The switch over from rifles, now termed "standard rifles" to distinguish them from assault rifles, came in the 1960s and 1970s but was born out of World War II. It was discovered that the vast majority of fire fights between infantry took place at ranges of 300 yards or less. Standard rifles were designed to be accurate at ranges of over 600 yards. As a consequence they were long–barreled and robust enough to cope with firing a large bullet with a powerful charge, but such long, heavy weapons proved to be an encumbrance to men fighting in trenches, buildings, and woodland.

Submachine guns evolved in an effort to solve this problem, but proved to be hopelessly inaccurate at ranges of more than 100 yards and they jammed frequently. The assault rifle was the answer.

US ARMY SOLDIERS armed with assault rifles on patrol with an Afghan security services soldiers in the summer of 2013. By the second decade of the 21st century assault rifles had become standard kit for the fighting soldiers of most states.

Changes to the Submachine Gun

In 1943 the Germans produced what they at first termed the MP43, designating it as a submachine gun. There were, however, important differences between this weapon and a standard submachine gun such as the MP40. The most obvious at first glance was the longer barrel and shoulder stock, but rather more important was the fact that it was chambered to take the 7.92x33mm cartridge. This fired a bullet that was comparable to that of the standard German army rifle, but had less propellant. This less-powerful charge meant the bullet had a shorter range, but it also put less pressure on the gun allowing a lighter weapon to be built. The weapon was deemed to be accurate to 400 yards, with a maximum range of 800 yards. Early trials led to some minor changes, and resulted in the MP44.

When the weapon went to Adolf Hitler for final approval, however, he suggested a new name was needed since the differences between this weapon and a submachine gun were so great. The name *Sturmgewehr* was settled on, which gave the new weapon the designation of StG44. The word *Sturmgewehr* literally means "storm rifle," but the more common English–language translation very early became "assault rifle" and the name has stuck.

MP44—KRUMMLAUF

This is a special edition of the MP44, the earlier designation for Germany's assault rifle the StG44. Although not immediately obvious in the profile view, this gun has a barrel that has been bent to enable the soldier using it to shoot around corners. The adaptation was known as the Krummlauf and came in different versions with different degrees of bend. This 30-degree bend is designated the StG Krummlauf I. As might be expected, the bent barrels had a very short lifespan, usually breaking after about 300 shots. Other problems included the tendency of the bullet to emerge from the barrel in a number of pieces giving an effect rather like firing a shotgun. Intended for infantry engaged in urban fighting, or for tank crews faced by concealed infantry, the Krummlauf was produced in only small numbers.

Bent barrel for shooting around corners

The trigger and pistol grip assembly was attached to the rest of the weapon by a hinged bolt that allowed the gun to be taken apart quickly and easily for field cleaning and maintenance.

BATTLE OF THE BULGE

The German assault rifle first came to the attention of the western Allies by its successful use in the Battle of the Bulge. This massive German offensive was unleashed on December 16, 1944. The main attack fell on the junction between the British and American Armies in northeastern France. The intention was to drive a wedge between the Allies, defeat each in turn and clear them out of Europe. The Germans could then turn their full force on the Russians and defeat them. The initial assault was a sweeping success as carefully coordinated attacks by panzers, artillery and infantry with the StG44 swept aside all resistance. After several days, however, the Allies were able to bring up massive reinforcements that first blunted and then halted the German attack. Good as it was, the StG44 could not cope with overwhelming enemy numbers.

The AK47

Possibly the 20th century's most important rifle, certainly one of the most widely used, the AK47 was Russia's answer to the German StG44. More than 60 years after it first entered service, it is still used the world over. The basic construction has remained the same, although a huge variety of versions and models exist. The original version, some 35 inches long, fired a 7.62x39mm cartridge at 100 rounds-per-minute on automatic settings (40 on semiautomatic) from a 30-round magazine. It was accurate to about 350 yards, though its maximum range was double that. It weighed only 7.7 pounds.

Skeleton metal stock reduced weight and allowed gun to be folded down to take up less space.

Butt on early versions made from wood

Space left around moving parts to minimize jamming

EARLY AK47

An early model AK47 with the original wooden butt and stamped metal components. A priority in the design process was that the weapon had to be easy to use and maintain when soldiers were wearing thick winter mittens to protect their fingers from the bitter cold of a Russian winter. The weapon was also expected to operate smoothly even when affected by dirt, mud, dust, or moisture—all of which were inevitable on campaign. The design featured generous clearances between moving parts to accommodate these demands, which led to a reduction in accuracy. This was considered to be a compromise worth making, and the extreme ruggedness and reliability of the AK47 on campaign or in inexperienced hands has become one of its most notable features.

Barrel was 16 inches long

Folding stock shortened gun by 10 inches

Stock folded sideways

AKS47

Folding metal stocks have been a feature of variant AK47s since its earliest days. In Russian these versions are dubbed the AKS47, where S stands for *skladnoy* or folding. The first AKS47 entered service in the 1950s and was intended for use by crew members of armored vehicles, particularly armored personnel carriers such as the BMP. Before long, folding stock versions were being produced for airborne troops with the designation AKMS. A number of variants were later produced with wooden stocks that folded sideways, as well as metal stocks that folded downward and plastic stocks that unclipped. The purpose of all these variants was to make the weapon shorter for use in confined spaces such as inside vehicles or aircraft, and also easier to store.

MIKHAIL KALASHNIKOV

Mikhail Kalashnikov, the inventor of the AK47, was born into a peasant family but as a teenager went to work in a tractor factory and discovered he had a talent for mechanics. He was conscripted into the Red Army in 1939 and in early 1942 he was wounded and sent back to hospital. While recuperating, he had the chance to study a submachine gun and began tinkering about with its design. This brought him to the attention of the Central Scientific bodies and he was given a job designing firearms. None of his early designs was adopted for production, but his innovations impressed his superiors. Finally in 1947 he produced the AK47 and his fame was assured. Kalashnikov went on to work on numerous variants and modernizations of his AK47, but also on machine guns and other weapons. After his retirement he made money licensing his name to be used on products such as hunting knives and vodka. He died in 2013.

Polymer shoulder stock includes flexible padding

Rail for attachment of telescopic sights

Forward grip gives added stability in automatic fire mode

The fore sight is based on that of the older Moson-Nagent with the addition of a fixed battle setting of 300 meters, the range at which the original version was expected to be most used.

Standard curved magazine holds 30 rounds, but optional drum magazine holds 100 rounds

MODERN AK47

Seen here is a modern AK47 variant with polymer fixtures. During the days of the Soviet Union, AK47s were not only distributed to Russian allies in large numbers, but instructions on manufacture were widely given out. The Soviets were happy for their allies and assorted Communist guerrilla groups to have easy access to this weapon as part of the wider conflict with the USA and capitalist governments. However, since the fall of the Soviet Union, the situation has changed. Realizing that they have a product of massive commercial appeal, the Izhevsk Machine Building Plant, which owns the patents, has been attempting to restrict who can manufacture AK47s and in what numbers. They have generally been successful in developed countries and with more modern variants, but older models are widely copied in countries that pay less attention to patents. Due to widespread copying over the years it is impossible to know how many AK47 guns have been made, but one estimate puts the number manufactured at around 100 million.

Submachine Guns

The formal definition of a submachine gun is that it is a weapon that uses the same continuous-fire mechanism of a machine gun, but that fires pistol ammunition. The type was introduced during World War I, but saw its greatest use in World War II when close quarters urban fighting made these especially useful weapons. However, submachine guns do have their limitations. They are generally not very accurate at ranges over 50 meters and are widely considered useless over 100 meters. The light ammunition they fire has little penetrating power and is easily thwarted by modern body armor.

Folding stock in folded position

Rudimentary rear sights

STERLING SUBMACHINE GUN
Experience of the wildly inaccurate Sten Gun prompted the British Army to issue a requirement for a submachine gun that would reliable hit a man-sized target at 100 yards. The result was the Sterling submachine gun that entered service just as World War II was ending and remained in service into the 1990s. The weapons could fire 550 rounds per minute of 9x19mm pistol ammunition, though one variant was designed to fire standard 7.62x51mm rifle ammunition. The gun achieved movie stardom when it featured in the first Star Wars trilogy as a "blaster" firing laser beams.

Suppressor

The Uzi pistol can be fitted with a suppressor that turns this into one of the quietest automatic weapons in the world, making it favored for clandestine operations.

Safety catch is released when pistol grip is squeezed

Magazine feeds through pistol grip

UZI SUBMACHINE GUN

The original Uzi was designed by Israeli army officer Uziel Gal in 1950 to be a personal-protection weapon for officers and rear-area troops such as truck drivers and service personnel. As such it was a great improvement on the pistols that had performed this function until then.

Cocking lever

Muzzle shroud helps dissipate heat

Muzzle of the Sterling produces a pronounced muzzle flash and louder report noise than is usual for submachine guns, making this weapon unsuitable for special forces and clandestine use. The basic blow-back open-bolt mechanism has since been used in a wide variety of variants of which some, such as the Uzi pistol shown here, are much smaller than the original. It is thought that over 10 million Uzis have been built, and the family of weapons remains in production.

The Cold War

Stretching from 1945 to 1990, the Cold War saw the world divided into three great power spheres. First came the Soviet Union and its Communist satellites, second the USA and its capitalist allies, and finally those other countries, often economically underdeveloped, which sought either to remain neutral or to take advantage of one or other of the hostile blocs as circumstances allowed. While the USA and the Soviet Union never went to war with each other, both became involved in small-scale conflicts or backed allies in wars by proxy. The weaponry used was often rudimentary and in the hands of badly trained militias, but at times could be extremely sophisticated and at the cutting edge of modern weaponry.

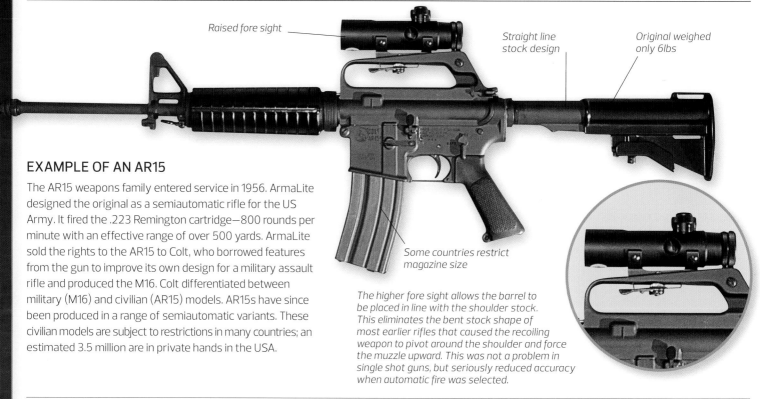

Raised fore sight

Straight line stock design

Original weighed only 6lbs

EXAMPLE OF AN AR15

The AR15 weapons family entered service in 1956. ArmaLite designed the original as a semiautomatic rifle for the US Army. It fired the .223 Remington cartridge—800 rounds per minute with an effective range of over 500 yards. ArmaLite sold the rights to the AR15 to Colt, who borrowed features from the gun to improve its own design for a military assault rifle and produced the M16. Colt differentiated between military (M16) and civilian (AR15) models. AR15s have since been produced in a range of semiautomatic variants. These civilian models are subject to restrictions in many countries; an estimated 3.5 million are in private hands in the USA.

Some countries restrict magazine size

The higher fore sight allows the barrel to be placed in line with the shoulder stock. This eliminates the bent stock shape of most earlier rifles that caused the recoiling weapon to pivot around the shoulder and force the muzzle upward. This was not a problem in single shot guns, but seriously reduced accuracy when automatic fire was selected.

M16 COLT M4

The M16 is the standard assault rifle of the US Army, and of several other armed forces around the world. It first entered service in 1962 when it was restricted to use in jungle combat zones, and entered other zones in 1970. It has undergone a number of upgrades and modifications. The gun can fire 900 rounds per minute in automatic setting; 45 rounds per minute in semiautomatic; or 15 rounds in single-shot mode. The magazine varies in size from 20 to 100 rounds, though the latter is considered to be too heavy for general use. The gun is accurate to 600 yards, and achieves reasonable success to 850 yards.

This example is the variant called M4

Picatinny rail enables it to carry range of sights and accessories

MP4's shorter barrel restricted to 3-round burst of fire

CHECKPOINT CHARLIE STANDOFF

By the summer of 1961, Germany had still not signed a formal peace treaty after the end of World War II. That meant that the four Allied Powers continued to administer Berlin on an ad hoc basis that saw the western powers occupying a large chunk of the city in the middle of Communist East Germany. Thousands of those who wished to flee Communist states in eastern Europe used Berlin as a way out. At midnight on August 12, 1961 the Russian President Khruschev closed the border with West Berlin and began the construction of what would become the Berlin Wall, while 32,000 troops marched into the city. US President John F. Kennedy mobilized US troops and moved them to West Germany. On October 22, as the tense standoff continued, a routine visit to East Berlin by an American diplomat was halted at Checkpoint Charlie by East German soldiers wielding AK47 assault rifles. Ten American tanks were brought up to lurk just out of sight of Checkpoint Charlie; the Soviets responded by bringing up 33 tanks. The commanders of both tank forces had orders to return fire and attack if fired upon. Frantic top-level talks between Kennedy and Khruschev followed. Three days later one of the Soviet tanks backed up 15 feet. An American tank did the same. Both forces then turned and drove away and the imminent threat of war departed.

Lightweight construction

6-shot magazine

AIRCREW'S "SURVIVAL RIFLE"

This cheap .22 rifle with a 6-shot magazine and lightweight construction was designed as a so-called "survival rifle" for aircrew during the 1950s by Harrington & Richardson Arms Co. of New York. It was designed to be carried in aircraft and would be used if the crew came down behind enemy lines. During the large number of irregular campaigns fought during the Cold War in Laos, Cambodia and elsewhere, US aircrews could find themselves faced by opponents who were none too scrupulous about applying the rules of war, so personal protection weapons such as this were common.

BATTLE OF THE IMJIN RIVER

In the spring of 1951 the Chinese decided to join the Korean War, supporting Communist North Korea against Capitalist South Korea which was in turn supported by a combined force of western powers. In April, 300,000 Chinese troops surged forward with the aim of capturing South Korea's capital Seoul. The attack began well, succeeding in pushing the southern allies back all along the line. However, the British Gloucestershire Regiment failed to pull back in time and was surrounded on an isolated hill overlooking the Imjin River. Although outnumbered by around 8 to 1 the Gloucesters held out for four days before they attempted to break out, though most were captured. The delay this inflicted on the Chinese advance meant they were unable to take the city of Seoul before American reinforcements arrived. Analysis of the battle revealed the limitations of the Gloucesters' SMLE rifles and prompted the British army to move toward universal use of assault rifles by the infantry.

Modern Assault Rifles

Once the assault rifle became established as the key infantry weapon of modern armies, designers began looking for ways to improve them so as to gain an edge of advantage over those weapons used by opponents. To this end during the 1970s there was a move toward smaller-caliber, higher-velocity ammunition.

The USA, for instance, abandoned the 7.62x51mm cartridge and instead adopted the 5.56x45mm, and soon others were following suit in moving to a caliber of only about 5mm. Trends during the 1980s were to adopt what became known as the

bullpup layout. This configuration put the gun action behind the trigger in what had previously been the butt stock. This resulted in a much shorter weapon while retaining the same barrel length. At about the same time, plastics and composite materials began to be used in gun construction. This in turn made it possible for the basic gun to become a platform for the addition of all sorts of modular add-on hardware such as laser sights, silencers, lights, and infra-red sights.

The 21st century has seen changes such as the introduction of multiple-caliber weapons and plastic-tipped bullets.

Telescopic buttstock

Able to carry modular add-ons

Box magazine holds 30 rounds

M4 CARBINE

The M4 carbine is a shorter, lighter version of the M16 rifle currently widely used by the US Military. It entered service in 1994 and has proved popular in action. The length is 33 inches with a 14.5-inch barrel. It is capable of firing 700 rounds per minute, but most examples are restricted to either semiautomatic or 3-round bursts. It is considered accurate to 600 yards and has a 30-round magazine holding the standard 5.56mm NATO cartridge.

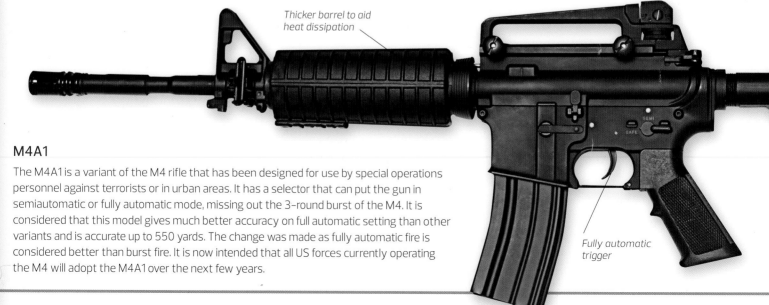

Thicker barrel to aid heat dissipation

Fully automatic trigger

M4A1

The M4A1 is a variant of the M4 rifle that has been designed for use by special operations personnel against terrorists or in urban areas. It has a selector that can put the gun in semiautomatic or fully automatic mode, missing out the 3-round burst of the M4. It is considered that this model gives much better accuracy on full automatic setting than other variants and is accurate up to 550 yards. The change was made as fully automatic fire is considered better than burst fire. It is now intended that all US forces currently operating the M4 will adopt the M4A1 over the next few years.

OPERATION GRANBY

The British contribution to the Gulf War of 1991 was given the name Operation Granby in honor of the famous British cavalry commander, the Marquis of Granby, who fought during the 18th century. Sea and air forces were involved, but the army operation was carried out largely by the 1st Armoured Division. The main punch of the division was in the form of Challenger tanks, but there were numerous mechanized infantry units, which traveled in Warrior armored personnel carriers. These men were armed with the SA80, Britain's standard infantry assault rifle.

Swarovski 1.5x telescopic and the Aimpoint CompM4 red dot are among sights that can be fitted to picatinny rail of the Steyr AUG

Barrel length 14.5 inches

Different sights can be fitted to rail

Picatinny rail above barrel

42-round magazine

STEYR AUG

The Austrian Steyr AUG assault rifle has been adopted by the Austrian, Australian, New Zealand and Saudi Arabian Armies, among others. It has the bullpup configuration, allowing it to be 31 inches long while having a 20 inch barrel. It features a progressive trigger, meaning that pulling the trigger halfway fires a single shot, while pulling it all the way gives fully automatic fire. This gets rid of the need for a selector but can result in automatic fire being produced when not intended. It is capable of 700 rounds per minute from its 42 round magazine and is accurate to 350 yards.

Collapsible butt stock

Barrel length 465mm

Pistol grip

M249

The M249 is officially classed as being a light machine gun, but its weight and portability put it on a near par with assault rifles and it is sometimes referred to as an assault weapon. The M249 entered service in 1984 in response to a perceived need for a squad of men to have the ability to lay down heavier fire than was possible with their assault rifles. The M249 is capable of up to 800 rounds per minute and is accurate up to 800 yards. The high rate of fire heats the barrel rapidly, so in action it is supplied with a replacement barrel, which can be swapped over rapidly. It is considered that the M249s in service are coming to the end of their lives due to heavy use, and so they are expected to be replaced before 2020.

MP5

Manufacturers Heckler & Koch designated the MP5 to be a submachine gun when it was introduced in 1966. Since then it has gone through a wide range of variants and upgrades, some of which are used more as assault rifles than submachine guns. Rate of fire is around 800 rounds per minute and range is about 150 yards. Magazine sizes vary from 15 to 100 in different versions. Originally intended for German border guards, federal police and other security forces, the MP5 has since been adopted by over 40 countries for both police and military uses.

The rear sight is adjustable for windage and for elevation and has four settings for different light conditions.

Fore hooded post sight

Rear rotary sight

Fire mode selector toggle

MP5K

The MP5K variant of the MP5 (see below left) was introduced with the aim of equipping special forces engaged on clandestine operations. The K designation comes from *kurz* or short, and well describes the variant. It has no shoulder stock and is designed to be fired with both hands holding handles. The bolt assembly was also shortened, to further lighten the gun and make it more compact. This version weighs only 4.4 pounds and is 14 inches long.

Barrel can be swapped when overheated

Fore sight

Flat end to receiver

Short muzzle means no suppressor can be fitted

Forward hand grip

Pistol grip

Magazine release toggle allows for swift removal and replacement of magazine.

BATTLE OF MAZAR-I SHARIF

The Battle of Mazar-i Sharif was the first major defeat for the Taliban in the Afghanistan War of 2001. The battle was fought between the Taliban (with Al Qaeda support and foreign volunteers) who were defending the city against an assault by Northern Alliance Afghans operating with American specialist support. The battle began on November 7, with American bombers pounding Taliban positions and supply routes. Two days later the ground offensive began. Outlying villages fell first, but by November 10, the city itself had fallen and the Taliban were in full retreat. The fighters on both sides were overwhelmingly equipped with secondhand assault rifles, mostly AK47s, although the small number of US special forces present carried MP5 submachine guns.

Sniping Rifles

Sniper Weapons

The art of killing an enemy from a distance is not new. In 1199, King Richard I of England was killed by a crossbow bolt which was shot at him when he thought himself out of range.

Before the advent of the rifle, however, the ability to hit a distant target lay with only an expert marksman. It was the advent of the rifle that made long-range sniping technologically possible for many more people.

Telescopic sights

AN AMERICAN SNIPER and his spotter aim at a target in Afghanistan in October 2006. The sniper is equipped with an M24SWS, which has an effective range of nearly a mile.

Guns Suitable for Sniping

Strictly speaking there is no such thing as a sniper rifle. The rifles used for sniping are simply guns that have the accuracy and range to be used for this purpose.

For most of the military history of the rifle, a sniper would use a standard model of a gun that he believed was more consistently accurate than other rifles. The accuracy of any particular gun reduces over time as the rifling grooves are worn away by the passage of bullets, so snipers have tended to replace their old guns with new ones fairly frequently. In recent years, some gun manufacturers have begun to build small numbers of rifles of exemplary design and finished with a high degree of precision, with a view to making them highly accurate over long ranges. So perhaps for the first time, a true sniper model is now in the process of being developed.

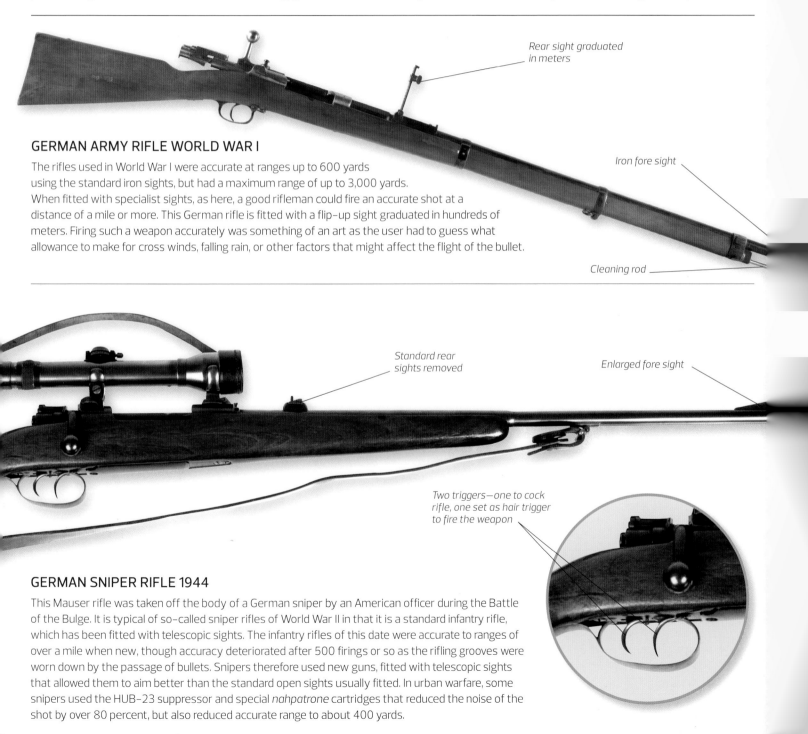

Rear sight graduated in meters

Iron fore sight

Cleaning rod

GERMAN ARMY RIFLE WORLD WAR I

The rifles used in World War I were accurate at ranges up to 600 yards using the standard iron sights, but had a maximum range of up to 3,000 yards. When fitted with specialist sights, as here, a good rifleman could fire an accurate shot at a distance of a mile or more. This German rifle is fitted with a flip-up sight graduated in hundreds of meters. Firing such a weapon accurately was something of an art as the user had to guess what allowance to make for cross winds, falling rain, or other factors that might affect the flight of the bullet.

Standard rear sights removed

Enlarged fore sight

Two triggers—one to cock rifle, one set as hair trigger to fire the weapon

GERMAN SNIPER RIFLE 1944

This Mauser rifle was taken off the body of a German sniper by an American officer during the Battle of the Bulge. It is typical of so-called sniper rifles of World War II in that it is a standard infantry rifle, which has been fitted with telescopic sights. The infantry rifles of this date were accurate to ranges of over a mile when new, though accuracy deteriorated after 500 firings or so as the rifling grooves were worn down by the passage of bullets. Snipers therefore used new guns, fitted with telescopic sights that allowed them to aim better than the standard open sights usually fitted. In urban warfare, some snipers used the HUB-23 suppressor and special *nahpatrone* cartridges that reduced the noise of the shot by over 80 percent, but also reduced accurate range to about 400 yards.

M40 MARINE SNIPER RIFLE

The sniper rifle currently used by the US Marine Corps is the M40, which first entered service in the M40A1 variant in 1966. It was the experience of the Vietnam War that convinced the Marines that they needed a sniper rifle. They bought several hundred Remington Model 40 rifles, and handed them over to Marine armorers Jack Cuddy and Neill Goddard to improve. The result was the M40. Over the years the weapon has gone through five official versions, though each of these has come with a variety of sights, silencers, and other additional features. Shown here is the M4A3, which entered service in 2001 and is now giving way to the M4A5. It has a specially made Schneider 24-inch, 6-groove barrel and the MST100 scope. It is generally reckoned to be accurate to 1,400 yards and comes with an internal 5-round magazine.

Notch in butt stock to allow rifle to be rested on a sandbag for additional stability

Sniper scope

Optional bipod barrel support

Schmidt & Bender 5–25x56 PM II LP telescopic sight

Optional suppressor

ACCURACY INTERNATIONAL AWM

The Accuracy International AWM takes its designation from the term "Arctic Warfare Magnum" but is not intended for Arctic warfare. The name came about because it was developed from British Army technology that is designed for use in very low temperatures. In fact, it can be used almost anywhere. The rifle comes in a variety of versions, but when chambered for the Lapua Magnum cartridge, it is classified as accurate to 1,600 yards and has a detachable 5-round magazine. Accuracy International, which manufactures the AWM, was founded in Britain 1977 by Olympic shooting gold medalist Malcolm Cooper and a team of fellow top international shooters. Their products are now in service with a number of armed forces, though their export is controlled by the British Government.

Monopod support

SIMO HAYHA

The record number of sniper kills for any one marksman was 505, credited to Simo Hayha, a Finnish sniper active during Finland's wars against the Soviet Union in the 1940s. Hayha used the M28 variant of the Russian Mosin-Nagant rifle, choosing to fire over basic iron sights instead of telescopic sights. To use the latter he would have had to lift his head, and the glass of such telescopic sights of the time was prone to fog up in cold weather. He operated by lying motionless in the snow of the Finnish winter wearing a set of white overalls, at times for hours on end, to hit a target. So deadly was Hayha—he was killing over 7 Russians a day at one point—that the Soviets called in artillery barrages and dedicated teams of snipers to try to kill him. Hayha was eventually hit by a Russian sniper and severely wounded, but he survived his injuries and lived on until 2002.

AWC G2

The AWC G2 is a specialist sniper rifle that has been produced in small numbers in the USA since the late 1990s. Details are confidential, but it is thought that fewer than 100 have been made. Lynn McWilliams and Gale McMillan worked together to produce what is generally recognized as being one of the finest sniper rifles ever produced. The 20-inch barrel and 20-round detachable box magazine are standard, but modular brackets allow for a wide range of sights, silencers, and other accessories to be fitted.

Telescopic sights mounted on rail for ease of change and replacement

Bullpup configuration

Padded shoulder butt stock

"Turret" on telescopic sight to adjust elevation

Elongated bolt to accommodate magnum cartridges

Box magazine holding 5 rounds

Rear monopod stock support

NEW SNIPER RECORD

In November 2009 British sniper Corporal Craig Harrison of the Household Cavalry and his spotters were in a sniping position at Musa Qala in Helmand Province of Afghanistan. The weather was crystal clear, mild, and dry, and there was no wind. They spotted two Taliban machine gunners in a nest at extreme range, even for the L115A3 variant of the AWM sniper rifle (see page 146). Harrison fired twice, killing the two Taliban fighters. The distance over which the shot was taken was later confirmed to be 2,707 yards—which set a new world record for a sniper shot.

ZASTAVA M76

Developed in Yugoslavia, and now used by the armed forces of the successor states, the Zastava M76 entered service in 1976. It was intended to be used by men of standard infantry units, allowing one or more men in a squad to achieve much better long-range accuracy than was normal for infantry without the specialized training and equipment of a true sniper. It has a range of about 900 yards and fires in a semiautomatic action from a detachable 10-round magazine. It has proved to be a rugged and reliable weapon, and saw extensive service in the wars that wracked the Balkans in the 1990s.

Cold-forged fluted barrel

Muzzle brake

Box magazine containing 10 rounds

Rubber pad on shoulder butt

HECATE

The standard sniper rifle of the French Army is the Hecate, which is also used by the armed forces of other European Union states. It has a range of about 1,900 yards and fires the 12.7x99mm Nato cartridge. It has a 7-round detachable magazine and a 27½-inch barrel. Unlike most sniper weapons the Hecate is not designed to kill people, instead it is designed to destroy equipment. The extremely heavy bullet that it fires is effective against vehicles, radar, aircraft, radios, artillery, and ammunition. The cartridges come in a variety of versions depending on the task in hand.

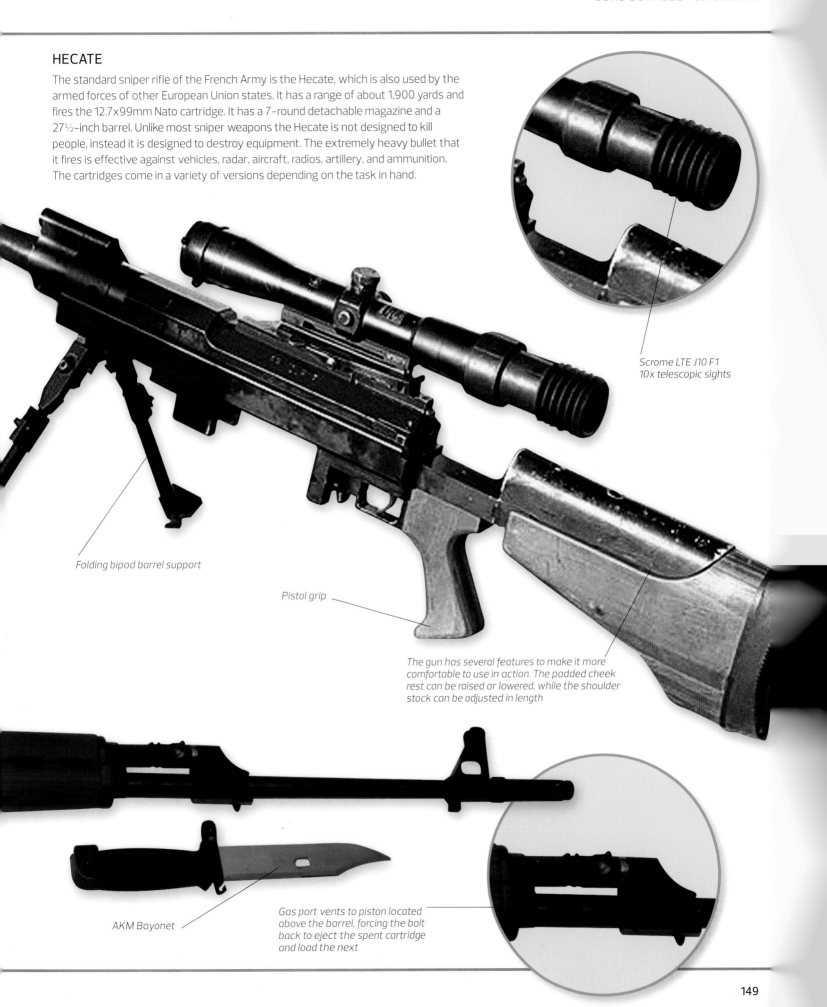

Scrome LTE J10 F1 10x telescopic sights

Folding bipod barrel support

Pistol grip

The gun has several features to make it more comfortable to use in action. The padded cheek rest can be raised or lowered, while the shoulder stock can be adjusted in length

AKM Bayonet

Gas port vents to piston located above the barrel, forcing the bolt back to eject the spent cartridge and load the next

Sporting Rifles

Rifles for Civilian Use

Rifles were originally developed for use as hunting weapons. In the days of black gunpowder, the grooves on a rifle were prone to get clogged after only a few shots were fired, which was a real disadvantage in battle situations. The improved accuracy of the rifle was of great use to a hunter, however, who might have only one worthwhile target in a day and wanted to be certain of hitting it. Rifles later moved on to the battlefield, but their prime use in civilian circles has remained for hunting.

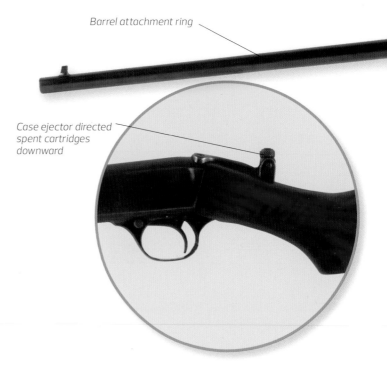

Barrel attachment ring

Case ejector directed spent cartridges downward

A DEER HUNTER at Accomack in Virginia shows off his prize and his AR15 K8 rifle, which is chambered to take the .243 Winchester Super Short Magnum cartridge.

Hunting Rifles

Hunting for food is probably the oldest use of weapons known to humanity. As soon as guns were invented, they were used for hunting and even today the vast majority of civilians are more likely to encounter a firearm that is used for hunting than any other type of gun. In most countries there are controls on hunting with guns. These restrict hunting to underpopulated areas and to certain seasons of the year. There are often restrictions on which guns can be used for what game animals, and some areas have limits on how many animals an individual can take in a given period of time. Modern hunting guns are so effective that these restrictions are necessary to safeguard potentially precarious animal populations.

Bolt in rear position to allow loading

3 chambers to take 3 cartridges simultaneously

BUFFALO MITRAILLE

Developed by Pierre Blachon in the 1890s, the Buffalo Mitraille was a French volley gun for small–game hunters. The barrel has three chambers running its entire length, and all three barrels are fired at once, using .22 ammunition. The concept was popular in France due to restrictions on the ownership of private firearms there from the 1880s to World War II, but it didn't catch on elsewhere.

Integral magazine

REMINGTON

Dating from 1941, this Model 24 semiautomatic .22 sporting rifle is based on a John Browning design. It is very similar to the Browning 22, which is still made today. It is a takedown design, meaning that the barrel separates easily from the rest of the weapon, making it simple to take apart for transportation. The Model 24 was made as a lightweight weapon so that it could be carried for long distances through rough country, without undue discomfort to the hunter using it.

DEER STALKING

In areas with no large predators, deer can breed prolifically to the point where they become a pest to humans (and deer populations suffer chronic health problems.) Culling is the process by which deer are hunted to maintain a steady population. Usually, licenses that allow hunters to take a specific number of males or females are issued, though in extreme cases unlimited licenses may be granted. In Britain, deer are hunted by stalking. This involves approaching the deer on foot, coming close enough to accurately identify individuals, so that the correct ones can be shot. In England, deer live mostly in forested areas and so stalking is done at dawn or dusk when the deer are more likely to venture on to farmland. In Scotland, however, the red deer live on open moorland and stalking takes place all day and often involves the hunter crawling through the heather to get close enough to take a shot. The deer stalker hat, made famous by Sherlock Holmes, has a long peak at the front to keep the sun out the eyes when aiming, and an identical peak at the back to stop rain dripping down inside the coat collar.

Modern Hunting Rifles

Over the past two decades hunting rifles have undergone something of a revolution as advanced technologies, which were previously limited to the military or the luxury end of the market, have become cheaper and more numerous, edging into the everyday hunting scene. It has become increasingly difficult for a layman to distinguish between a civilian hunting weapon and a military one. One of the most obvious of these innovations is the use of polymers for components in place of metal. These were first used only in the stock, but in more recent years have also been found in the actual receiver and operating parts.

Almost as important in terms of the look of a rifle is the new straight-through layout, which allows the shoulder stock to be in a straight line with the barrel. This reduces the tendency of the muzzle to jerk up with recoil when the gun is fired, and is made possible by having iron sights set high.

Straight-line configuration – from barrel to butt stock

Polymer butt stock

Pistol grip

BUSHMASTER DISSIPATOR

Bushmaster was founded in North Carolina in 1973 by the Freedom Group conglomerate that also includes Remington. Most Bushmaster rifles are variants based on the military M4 carbine, which the company produced for the US military. The Bushmaster Dissipator was introduced as an effort to combine a short carbine barrel with the longer sights of a rifle. The early version suffered from problems caused by variations in the gas pressure of the ammunition affecting the gas-operated semiautomatic loading system. These problems have been fixed by later variants.

The fore sight is mounted above the gas port to give the greatest possible distance between rear sight and fore sight. This increases the accuracy of aiming over iron sights, but means that care must be taken when handling the fore sight to avoid damage to the gas port.

Magazine release catch

Polymer barrel shroud

OLYMPIC ARMS K22

The Olympic K22 is another of the many weapons based on the AR-15 now on the market. It was the first of a family of similar weapons firing a rimfire .22 cartridge. The weapon has a one-piece barrel with the appropriate chamber-end machined right into the barrel. The stock and other fittings on the K22 are made of composite plastics and epoxies produced by Fiberite, a South African company that began making plastic manhole covers but which now makes specialist components for Formula 1 cars and weapons worldwide.

MAINTENANCE

Before the advent of modern materials and mechanisms into the world of sport and hunting shooting, maintaining a hunting weapon was usually a fairly straightforward business. A minimum of equipment was needed, often no specialist tools were required at all, and most guns could be stripped down, cleaned and reassembled in the field. The more modern weapons, however, require more care. A typical AR-15, for instance, requires specialist maintenance tools and some of the parts are so small that the procedure should best be done on a clean surface in a sheltered site. The AR-15 magazine cannot be taken apart for cleaning, so when it becomes too fouled for safe use, it has to be discarded.

COLT SPORTER SP1

The Colt Sporter is marketed as a hunting weapon and as such has a number of features that have been incorporated to bring it into line with hunting legislation in various states within the USA, such as having a magazine limited to holding only five rounds. The gun comes in two basic versions, the "Competition" with a 20-inch barrel and overall weight of 8.5 pounds, and the "Lightweight" with a 16-inch barrel and weight of 7.2 pounds, though there are a number of other variations on the market.

Straight-stock configuration

Fore sight

Rear sight

The standard rear sight is in the rear of the carrying handle and can be adjusted for windage and elevation. A range of telescopic sights can be mounted on top of the handle

Pistol grip

Stock made of composite plastics and epoxies

Magazine

About the Berman Museum

Since the Berman Museum of World History opened its doors to the public in April of 1996, thousands of visitors have enjoyed its unique and varied collection of art, historical objects, and weapons. Located in the Appalachian foothills in Anniston, Alabama, and next door to the 75-year-old Anniston Museum of Natural History, which is affiliated with the Smithsonian, the Berman Museum's reputation and collection have grown exponentially since its inception. The Berman Museum's holdings number 8,500 objects and it has 3,000 items related to world history exhibited in its galleries. Among the many rare and fascinating objects from around the world, there are items such as an air rifle from Austria, military insignia from German and Italy, a scimitar from the Middle East, and graphically carved kris holders from Indonesia. The Museum attracts both a global and regional audience. All who visit can appreciate the historic significance of the collection and gain greater awareness and respect of other cultures.

Its five galleries—Deadly Beauty, American West, World War I, World War II, and Arts of Asia—exhibit items spanning a period of 3,500 years. A focal point of the Deadly Beauty gallery is the elaborate Royal Persian Scimitar, circa 1550, created for Abbas the Great, King of Persia. The American West gallery covers approximately 200 years (c. 1700–1900), emphasizing the United State's political, economic, social, and cultural structures, and their influences on settling the West.

The World War galleries use objects from the Museum collection to explore the causes and conditions of both wars, the historical significance of the countries involved, and the resulting political, economic, cultural, and social changes brought about by each war.

A rare piece of equipment in the World War I gallery is the Tanker's Splinter Goggles, used by tank personnel to protect their eyes and faces from metal splinters from machine-gun fire. Exhibited in the World War II gallery is the M1942 "Liberator" Pistol, as well as a large collection of Adolf Hitler's tea and coffee service, purported to have come from the last bunker that the Führer occupied. The Arts of Asia exhibit features an extensive and ever-growing collection of Asian textiles, ceramics, sculpture, jade, and metal.

The Berman Museum of World History is home to the vast and eclectic collection of Colonel Farley L. Berman and his wife, Germaine. Farley Berman, a lifelong resident of Anniston, Alabama, served in the European theater during World War II, and in the occupation force afterward. There he met Germaine, a French national. They were married and spent the next 50 years traveling the world acquiring historic weapons and artifacts, paintings, bronzes, and other works of art. Berman's self-trained collector's eye recognized the importance of items that were perhaps seen as ordinary, and he made it his mission to preserve a few. The Bermans established contacts—and a reputation—in numerous auction houses and among antique dealers in Europe and America.

The Bermans freely shared their collection with the public long before the City of Anniston constructed the Museum facility. Hundreds of military dignitaries and others were invited to their home for personal tours of their collection. Colonel Berman could best be described as a colorful storyteller and was notorious for firing blank rounds from his collection of spy weapons when guests least expected. He advised aspiring collectors to purchase good reference books, spend some years reading, and visit a range of museums before acquiring.

During the early 1990s, several large museums expressed interest in receiving the Bermans' collection. They were disappointed when Germaine proposed that the collection remain in Anniston. Colonel and Mrs. Berman's collection stands as the core of Berman Museum. Since the Museum's opening, many have recognized its importance and have contributed their own personal treasures to this impressive collection.

Glossary of Rifle Terms

A

Action Generally speaking, the overall firing mechanism of a gun

Arquebus Shoulder-fired matchlock musket

Assault rifle A rifle capable of firing single shots, bursts, or fully automatic fire, and which uses a less powerful cartridge than a battle rifle

B

Ball A synonym for bullet

Bayonet A dagger, knife, or sword that is attached to the muzzle of a rifle

Blunderbuss A short, smoothbore musket (occasionally a pistol) with a flared muzzle to spread shot over a wider area

Bolt In reference to crossbows, a short dartlike projectile, also known as a *quarrel*

Bolt-action A gun (typically a rifle) whose action is operated by manipulating a bolt, either by drawing it back ("straight pull") or on a rotational axis

Bore *See Gauge*

Buckshot Lead pellets fired by shotguns

Butt, or Buttstock The part of a gun braced against the shoulder for firing

C

Caliber The diameter of a cartridge, expressed in fractions of an inch (e.g., .38, .45) or millimeter (e.g., 7.62mm, 9mm)

Carbine A short-barreled, compact musket or rifle, originally carried by mounted troops or, in modern times, by soldiers whose primary jobs (vehicle crews, for example) made it impractical to carry a full-size rifle

Cartridge The cased combination of bullet, powder, and primer used in modern firearms; prior to the introduction of the metallic cartridge, the term referred to bullet and powder wrapped in paper for ease of loading muzzle-loading weapons

Center-fire A type of cartridge with the primer sealed in a cavity in the center of its base

Chamber The part of a gun in which the cartridge is seated before firing

Chassepot 19th-century French bolt-action rifle

Clip A metal strip holding a number of cartridges for insertion into a gun

D

Darra guns Guns produced by the gunsmiths of Darra adem Khel (then part of India, now part of Pakistan)

Deringer The original weapons made by Henry Deringer; the imitation was spelled with an additional "r"

Derringer Short, extremely compact and concealable pistol

Double-action A gun (either revolver or automatic) in which a single, long trigger pull both fires the weapon and brings a cartridge into the chamber in readiness for firing. *See also Single-action*

F

Firing pin The part of a gun's firing mechanism that strikes the cartridge's primer

Flintlock Gun-firing system utilizing a piece of flint striking against a piece of steel to strike sparks for ignition

G

Gas-operated Term used to describe a gun that taps excess gas from the weapon to operate the action

Gatling gun A multi-barreled gun fed from a hopper, developed during the American Civil War and still in use in an electrically operated version

Gauge For shotguns, the equivalent of the term "caliber," in this case expressed as fractions of a pound, e.g., 12-gauge; synonymous with *Bore*

Grip General term for the handle of a sword, knife, or bayonet.

H

Handgun Originally used to refer to any firearm that could be carried and used by an individual; in modern usage it refers solely to pistols

Hilt The portion of a sword grasped by the user, usually consisting of the guard, grip, and pommel

L, M

Lever-action A gun that uses a lever, pushed downward and then upward by the firer, to load and eject cartridges

Magazine The part of a gun containing cartridges in readiness for firing; in rifles, the magazine is often charged (loaded) by a clip

Matchlock Early firearms which used a slow-burning match to provide ignition

Musket Generally, a smoothbore, shoulder-fired infantry weapon, in use in the West up until the widespread introduction of rifles in the mid-19th century

Musketoon A short-barreled musket

Muzzle The opening of a gun's barrel

Muzzle-loading Used to refer to a gun that loads by the muzzle

P, Q

Percussion cap A capsule containing a fulminating agent that explodes when struck sharply. When fitted to a firearm a percussion cap will ignite the main charge of gunpowder even in wet weather

Picatinny rail Mounting platform on some firearms for attachments and accessories such as sights

Pinfire An early type of self-contained cartridge, no longer in common use

Primer The part of a cartridge which, when struck by the firing pin, ignites and fires the main charge

Pump-action A gun whose action is operated by a sliding mechanism, usually mounted below the barrel

Quarrel *See Bolt*

R

Receiver Generally speaking, the part of a gun incorporating the action, as distinct from the stock and barrel

Recoil The backward pressure exerted when a gun is fired

Recoil-operated A type of semi- or fully automatic gun that uses recoil to operate the action

Rifle A firearm that is designed to be fired from the shoulder, with a barrel that has a helical groove or grooves (*rifling*) cut into the barrel walls

Rifling The process of boring cylindrical grooves into a gun barrel to stabilize the bullet in flight, thus increasing accuracy

Rimfire A type of cartridge in which the primer is evenly distributed around the rear of the base

Round Synonym for cartridge, usually used to refer to magazine capacity, e.g., twenty-round.

S

Sabre Curved sword typically used by cavalry

Safety The part of a gun's action designed to prevent accidental firing

Self-loading Used to refer to guns that will fire once with each trigger pull without the need to reload; the term is synonymous with *Semiautomatic*

Semiautomatic *See Self-loading*

Shotgun Smoothbore, shoulder-fired weapon, typically firing buckshot; most commonly used in hunting but also in combat

Single-action A revolver that has to be manually cocked before each shot; single-action automatics require cocking only before the first shot is fired; *see also Double-action*

Smoothbore A gun with an unrifled barrel. *See Rifling*

Snaphance, Snaphaunce A type of lock, an ancestor of the *Flintlock*

Sniper A marksman who kills an enemy or destroys weapons or equipment from a distance (usually from a distance considered beyond the range of conventional rifles fired by average marksmen)

Stock Any part of a gun which is gripped with the hand before firing; *see also Butt*

Submachine gun A gun that combines the automatic fire of a machine gun with the cartridge of a pistol

T

Torador A *matchlock* musket that was used in India for hundreds of years

Touchhole The opening in early firearms and cannons through which the powder was ignited

Trigger The part of a gun's action pulled back by the firer's finger to discharge the weapon

W

Wheel lock Firing mechanism that used the friction of a spring-powered metal wheel against iron or flint for ignition

Index

Acknowledgments

Moseley Road Inc would like to thank the following people for their assistance and patience in the making of this book: **The Berman Museum of World History**: Adam Cleveland, David Ford, Susan Doss, Evan Prescott, Sara Prescott, Quinton Turner, and Kira Tidmore

Picture Credits

Unless otherwise noted, all silhouetted weaponry images are from the Berman Museum of World History, Anniston, Alabama, and photographed by *f*-stop fitzgerald and Jonathan Conklin Photography, Inc., with the exception of the following:

KEY : a above, b below, l left, r right, c center, t top

Covert and coverb Merz Antique Firearms, merzantiques.com; pp8–9, 10l Duncan1890/istock 13br Library of Congress, LC-USZ62-33515 17t Ironholds at en.wikipedia 19b Georges Jansoone 20t Rama 21tr HuttyMcphoo 30–31, 32l Library of Congress, LC-DIG-pga-02211 37b MatthewVanitas 40–41, 42l Library of Congress, LC-DIG-pga-03235 44t Library of Congress, LC-DIG-pga-04033, restored by Adam Cuerden 55 Courtesy of Rock Island Auction Company 57t Library of Congress, LC-USZC4-7934 60–61, 62l Buffalo Bill Historical Center 71b Library of Congress, LC-USZC4-7160 76–77, 78l meunierd/ Shutterstock 80b Armémuseum 81t Wasily 82b Marafona/ Shutterstock 87br Armémuseum 87t RJ Militaria 86–87c Canadian War Museum 88t Armémuseum 88b P Mateus 89 NARA 90t Armémuseum 90c Antique Military Rifles 90b C&Rsenal 91c Courtesy of Rock Island Auction Company 91b Armémuseum 92t MKFI 92bl Shussho 93t MKFI 93b George Shuklin 95tr The National Library of Scotland 96t Rama 100–101c

Edmond Huet 103bl Bundesarchiv, Bild 101III-Zschaeckel-206–35/Zschäckel, Friedrich 107t Imperial War Museum 108ca Damien Peter Parer, Australian War Memorial 108b PHGCOM 113t Olemac/Shutterstock 113b Zimand/ Shutterstock 114a Army Heritage Museum Collection 116cl Staff Sergeant Louis R. Lowery, USMC 122b Manxruler 123c Gerd 72 123t Andrew Bossi 128–129, 130l U.S. Navy/Mass Communication Specialist 2nd Class Ace Rheaume 132b vadim kozlovsky/ Shutterstock 134–135b, 135a CreativeHQ/Shutterstock 136t M62 136b TV-PressPass 138t S-F/Shutterstock 138b Vartanov Anatoly/Shutterstock 139 Rodionov/Shutterstock 140t Zimand/ Shutterstock 140b Vartanov Anatoly/Shutterstock 141 Zimand/ Shutterstock 142–143, 144l Cpl Bertha Flores, US Army 146t Gunnery Sgt Matt Hevezi, USMC 146–147b Andrew Linnett/ Defence Imagery 148b uzz75 149t davric 150–151, 152l Olympics Arms Inc 154t Budsgunshop.com 155b